COOKING
for TWO
TODAY

Jean Hewitt
Marjorie Page Blanchard

LITTLE, BROWN AND COMPANY
Boston   Toronto   London

DEDICATION

This book is written in memory of
Marjorie Page Blanchard,
a good friend and respected colleague.

FIRST PAPERBACK EDITION

Library of Congress Cataloging-in-Publication Data

Hewitt, Jean.
  Cooking for two today.

  Includes index.
  1.Cookery. I. Blanchard, Marjorie P. II. Title.
TX652.H47   1985   641.5'61   85-7839
ISBN 0-316-35979-3 (hc)
ISBN 0-316-35991-2 (pb)

10   9   8   7   6   5   4   3

MV-NY

Designed by Patricia Girvin Dunbar

Published simultaneously in Canada
by Little, Brown & Company (Canada) Limited

PRINTED IN THE UNITED STATES OF AMERICA

CONTENTS

INTRODUCTION v

APPETIZERS 1

SOUPS 13

FISH 29

POULTRY 51

MEATS 85

MEATLESS MAIN DISHES 117

VEGETABLES 127

SALADS 153

RICE AND PASTA 173

SAUCES, FILLINGS, AND ACCOMPANIMENTS 185

DESSERTS 195

INDEX 213

INTRODUCTION

The empty-nest syndrome happened in my home more than a decade ago and, at first, the switch to cooking for two was traumatic, with leftovers at every meal. After a while, it became frustrating enough to force me to concentrate on shopping for two at the supermarket and the cookware store. I have gradually accumulated a collection of tried and true recipes to serve two, with menus for all seasons that will work for two-member households of all ages. When the question came up about taking over the project on Cooking for Two that my friend the late Marjorie Blanchard had started, I was delighted to accept the assignment.

QUICK AND LIGHT

The recipes in this book are easy to follow; they do not require complicated techniques, and they produce great-tasting dishes that fit today's preference for healthful, lighter eating. Even though I enjoy cooking and find it relaxing, a demanding full-time job and hobbies such as tennis and gardening make it imperative that my meals for two go together fast. This requirement is reflected in the book by over fifty dinner menu suggestions that can be prepared in thirty minutes or less. At certain times, usually on weekends, I am ambitious enough to fix a double quantity of a dish that requires long cooking, such as Braised Lamb Shanks or Braised Turkey Drumsticks. I build up a cache of main dishes for two in the freezer; thawed slowly overnight in the refrigerator, they are ready to reheat the following evening.

The arrangement of the chapters in this book is traditional in that it goes from appetizers to desserts, but there are one or two gaps and shifts of emphasis. I seldom bake yeast or quick breads unless guests are expected because there are so many good commercial products available that reflect the trend to whole grains with no preservatives. Quality whole-wheat pita and Italian bread and even all-butter croissants can be found with a little effort.

The balance of one-third fish recipes to one-third poultry and one-third meat (beef, pork, ham, lamb and veal) also mirrors a healthy trend. In my home we eat even less meat, but I suspect that is because we have access to super-fresh fish from local waters that can be cooked quickly with little fuss.

This conscious choice of fish and poultry as the main protein source for dinner reduces the total fat, and therefore calories and cholesterol. I try to keep fat additions to a minimum by using low-fat dairy products, such as yogurt and skim milk, and I cut down on butter and oil. I have experimented with vegetable sprays in no-stick pans, to replace fat or oil for sautéing and browning, but I do not like the results. Better to walk an extra mile, or play an extra set of tennis, than eliminate all the added fat. This is a cookbook for healthful eating, not dieting, and once in a while I splurge on a small quantity of cream where I think the quality of the end product demands it. There are few sauce recipes because I seldom find them necessary with the lighter way of cooking and eating.

In recent years I have become sensitive to salty foods and have gradually adjusted my cooking so that I do not add salt automatically. I have increased other flavor elements such as herbs, especially fresh from the garden, spices, lemon juice, and vinegar, and I taste toward the end of the cooking time to decide whether salt is needed. Most of the time it is not. Certainly when salty ingredients are called for, such as canned broth, capers, cheese, soy sauce, celery, and anchovies, I never add salt in cooking. In the book I have left the choice, and amount, to the cook's conscience. If you are just becoming aware of too much salt in your diet, reduce the amount gradually and you will barely notice the loss.

Major food processors are starting to acknowledge the trend to reducing the salt in the diet and it is possible to purchase no-salt-added, and reduced salt, canned tomato, vegetable, and soup products. I have found most of them to be highly acceptable and worth their higher cost. I recommend their use in the recipes in this book.

I use home-canned, with no salt added, tomatoes and always unsalted butter; I do not keep any other kind in the house.

Fruit of the season is the dessert I prefer but, to satisfy my husband's sweet tooth, I keep a few goodies such as Frozen Orange Mousse, Frozen Chocolate Dessert and Apple Almond Tarts in the freezer. I also find them handy when inviting guests on the spur of the moment. I splurged on buying an ice-cream machine that has its own refrigeration unit, and requires no ice or salt, and I enjoy experimenting with fruit ices and sherberts. However, I have not included those recipes in this book as it would be frustrating for those who do not own the equipment.

EQUIPMENT

My major investment for cooking for two was a larger toaster oven because I resented turning on the regular oven to bake a couple of salmon steaks or apple crisp for two. Many of the recipes in this book suggest the use of a toaster oven. I invested in a set of top-quality, small saucepans with covers, ranging from one-pint to two-quart capacities; two eight-inch skillets, one cast iron and the other heavy aluminum. In cooking for two, I use two- and three-quart heavy casseroles of porcelainized iron for soups, stews and braised meats and a large kettle for pasta, lobster and other shell fish. My most useful freezer-to-oven-(or-microwave)-to-table dishes are earthenware, oval au gratin dishes measuring 6 by 3⅓ inches on the bottom and with a capacity of about 1½ cups. Also, I have a medium-size roasting pan with a rack, a loaf pan, a one-quart soufflé dish, and individual six-ounce ramekins.

My kitchen has measuring cups for dry ingredients, measuring spoons, and graduated glass measuring cups for liquids. Food preparation for two requires a colander, large and small strainers, a metal funnel, bulb baster, ten- and eight-ounce custard cups (about six of each), a set of mixing bowls, a vegetable brush, whisk, a large spoon, spatula, pancake turner, timer. (Smaller whisks, wooden spoons and spatulas are easier for cooking for two.) I use only freshly ground pepper from a pepper mill. I prefer a salad spinner for drying lettuce, spinach, and parsley and I have a good quality pair of kitchen shears. They can be used for everything from snipping chives and dill to cutting pizza slices and chicken parts.

If you plan to make pastry, invest in a wooden board and rolling pin. I do not like cloth covers for either, but if you intend to make the dough from scratch, a wire pastry blender is helpful and a flour sifter is essential. An egg slicer makes neat slices for garnishes. Knives must be top quality, and sharpened regularly, and include a paring knife with a sharp pointed end, a serrated tomato slicer, at least three sizes of chef's style French knives, a boning knife, a bread knife, a ham slicer, and a carving set. To the cutlery drawer I would add a potato peeler, tongs a meat thermometer, an oven thermometer, a can opener, a corkscrew, and a pastry brush. I have two pickle crocks, one on either side of my range; one is filled with wooden spoons, spatulas, brushes, whisks, large spoons, and so forth, and the other with baking tools such as the rolling pin, spatulas, pastry brushes and pot holders.

Aluminum foil pans sold in all supermarkets and variety stores include individual tart pans and baking dishes, and I keep a selection on hand. A hand (or stand) electric mixer, a blender, and a food processor are on my kitchen counter and used frequently. Three appliances that I enjoy, but am not a slave to, are a microwave oven, a countertop convection oven, and a chest freezer. Some of the recipes in this book can be adapted for microwave cooking.

BASIC EQUIPMENT FOR TWO

APPLIANCES

Toaster oven	Electric mixer
Microwave oven	Food processor or blender

POTS AND PANS

Set of sauce pans with covers (different sizes)	Medium-size roasting pan with rack
Eight-inch cast-iron skillet	Loaf pan

Eight-inch heavy aluminum skillet   Large kettle

Two-quart heavy casserole
  of porcelainized iron
Three-quart heavy casserole
  of porcelainized iron
One-quart soufflé dish

Set of six-ounce ramekins
Six eight-ounce custard
  cups
Six ten-ounce custard cups

Set of mixing bowls
Graduated glass measuring
  cup
Colander
Large strainer

Small strainer
Metal funnel
Flour sifter
Salad spinner
Wooden board

Measuring spoons
Bulb baster
Vegetable brush
Whisk
Wooden spoons
Spatula
Pancake turner

Rolling pin
Kitchen shears
Wire pastry blender (op-
  tional)
Pastry brush
Meat thermometer
Oven thermometer

Paring knife
Serrated tomato slicer
Three sizes of French
  knives
Boning knife

Bread knife
Carving set
Potato peeler
Can opener
Egg slicer

Timer	Peppermill
Corkscrew	Tongs

SHOPPING

I shop once a week, early on Saturday morning, and I plan a week's worth of menus in my head. However, the plan is flexible enough to allow for good-looking specials at the market, unexpected guests, and eating out at a restaurant once in a while. I keep a running list of staples that need to be replenished.

My shopping, bulk cooking, and freezing are done in the country, at my weekend home, and I carry prepared foods and raw ingredients back to the city in insulated containers with ice packs. I find the convenience, and the savings in time and money during the work week, worth the effort.

The first stop on Saturday is always the fish shop; being close to the ocean, we are fortunate to be able to buy really top-quality fresh fish. One week it might be Block Island swordfish to cook on the grill, mussels, and haddock. Another time scrod, flounder, and steamers. We eat, and serve to guests, fish on most Saturdays and Sundays. It is a snap to prepare and we have come to appreciate lighter foods. I never waste leftover fish; it goes into Kedgeree or I marinate it in Vinaigrette Dressing overnight for a great luncheon or dinner salad.

A relatively small, independent supermarket is my second shopping stop because they have excellent fresh produce in bulk so I can pick and choose exactly the size and quantity I need. I buy what is in season and looks good, and fill in with year-round available items. We are big salad eaters, so it is not unusual for me to buy heads of Boston, romaine, and leaf lettuce. Except in the summer, when I have home-grown tomatoes and cucumbers, I prefer European-style cucumbers and cherry tomatoes. They have more flavor. We eat a lot of fresh spinach in salads and cooked spinach as a vegetable and as an ingredient in many dishes. During the asparagus season, we will have it two or more times a week, and then I am happy to wait for the next season to roll around. This philosophy is true with most other fresh fruits and vegetables.

I usually buy meat for one braised, or stewed, dish, such as Veal Stew with Mushrooms and maybe Meat Balls, and I cook them during the weekend and either freeze or refrigerate, depending on when I plan to serve them. I buy chicken breasts to skin, bone, and use in a quick sauté dish. I freeze ground lamb and lean ground beef in patties with wax paper between for quick thawing and using in such recipes as Ground Lamb with Feta Cheese and Spinach and tacos. I always have ground turkey in the freezer for Turkey Chili or Enchiladas. I buy a slice of ham, smoked pork chops or roasted turkey breast in cryovac packaging which will keep until Thursday, the last night we eat in the city.

The only dessert we eat during the week is fresh fruit. We enjoy soups all year round; often cold cucumber or squash in summer, with home-grown vegetables and lots of fresh herbs, and heartier bean and lentil varieties in the winter. I make a double quantity on the weekend for lunch and carry leftovers back to the city in insulated containers to enjoy during the week.

I always have Well-Seasoned Tomato Sauce and pesto in the freezer for quick pasta meals, with or without meat or clams. I keep a cache of frozen desserts in the country, which are a boon when I'm faced with unexpected guests.

STAPLES

Following is a list of basic supplies for a well-stocked kitchen:

DAIRY

1 quart skim milk	2 sticks unsalted butter or
6 eggs	margarine
wedge Parmesan cheese	wedge Cheddar cheese

PRODUCE

1 pound carrots

1 bulb garlic

1 head celery

6 yellow onions

2 lemons

BAKING

All-purpose unbleached
flour

Confectioners' sugar

Cornstarch

Baking soda

Cornmeal

Unflavored gelatin

Shortening

Vegetable oil

Granulated sugar

Light brown sugar

Baking powder

Cream of tartar

Long-grain or converted
rice

Unflavored dry bread
crumbs

FLAVORINGS

Olive oil

Honey

Worcestershire sauce

Catsup

Cider vinegar

Dry white wine

Dijon-style mustard

Mayonnaise

Canned chicken and beef
broth (preferably low-
salt)

No-salt-added tomato sauce,
paste and tomatoes

Sesame seeds

Preserves

Dried lentils and split peas

Black peppercorns

Paprika

Chili powder

Curry powder

Leaf thyme

Leaf oregano

Leaf marjoram

Bay leaves

Ground cinnamon

Ground ginger

Caraway seeds

Whole cloves

Almond extract

Maple syrup

Soy sauce

Liquid hot pepper seasoning

Wine vinegar

Vermouth

Country-style mustard
Frozen chopped chives
Raisins
Pasta (several shapes)
Salt
Cayenne pepper
Dry mustard
Crushed red peppers
Leaf sage

Leaf tarragon
Leaf basil
Leaf rosemary
Ground nutmeg
Ground cumin
Ground coriander
Cinnamon sticks
Vanilla

METRIC CONVERSION TABLE

AMERICAN   METRIC

LIQUID

1 teaspoon	5 milliliters
1 tablespoon (3 teaspoons)	15 milliliters
1 cup (16 tablespoons or 8 fluid ounces)	250 milliliters
1 quart (4 cups)	1 scant liter
1 gallon (4 quarts)	3.7 liters

DRY MEASURE

1 ounce	28 grams
1 pound	450 grams
3½ ounces	100 grams
2 pounds 3 ounces	1 kilo (1,000 grams)

TABLE OF EQUIVALENTS

Bread crumbs, soft	1 cup	2 slices
Bread cubes	1 cup	2 slices
Cheese		
Cheddar or Swiss	1 pound shredded	4 cups
Parmesan	¼ pound grated	1¼ cups

Eggs

whole	1 cup	5 to 6
yolks	1 cup	13 to 14
whites	1 cup	7 to 8

Flour

all-purpose	1 pound sifted	4 cups
cake	1 pound sifted	4¾ to 5 cups

Pasta

elbow macaroni or spaghetti	½ pound uncooked	4 cups cooked

Rice

regular white	1 cup raw yields	3 cups cooked
converted	1 cup raw yields	4 cups cooked
brown	1 cup raw yields	4 cups cooked

Fruits and Vegetables

Apples	1 pound	3 medium-size
Lemons	1 medium grated	2 teaspoons rind
	1 medium squeezed	2 tablespoons juice
Oranges	1 medium grated	2 tablespoons rind
	1 medium squeezed	⅓ to ½ cup juice
Carrots	1 pound sliced	2½ cups
Cabbage	1 pound shredded	4 cups
Herbs	1 tablespoon chopped fresh	1 teaspoon dried
Onions	1 pound yellow	5 to 6 medium-size
Potatoes	1 pound all-purpose	3 medium-size
Mushrooms	1 pound sliced	3 cups
Tomatoes	1 pound	3 medium-size

MENUS

Throughout this cookbook, accompaniments have been suggested for nearly every main dish. And most recipes carry a symbol identifying their special characteristics (easy to double, can be frozen, can be made ahead, quick, seasonal, versatile, and good for using up leftovers). The reader can therefore find a menu suitable for the requirements of any meal.

For your additional convenience, complete menus are provided here for the two kinds of meals that need them most: elegant occasions, and the bane of the two-person family: efficient use of leftovers.

ELEGANT

These menus are also great for doubling when company comes.

Gazpacho*
Roast Cornish Game Hen*
Wild Rice*
Mushroom Salad*
Apple Almond Tarts*

Roast Duck with Fruit
  Stuffing and Sauce*
Wild Rice*
Brussels Sprouts and Chest-
  nuts*
Strawberry Mousse*

Rhode Island Clam Chow-
  der*
Scallops in White Wine*
Sautéed julienned zucchini
Frozen Orange Mousse*

Herbed Cheese* in mush-
  room caps
Sole Kiev*
New potatoes
Broccoli Puree*
Endive and Beet Salad*
Melon balls

Pork Cutlets Normandy*
Scalloped Potatoes*
Ratatouille*
Green salad
Flambéed Bananas*

*Recipe in book

LEFTOVER COMBINATIONS

ONE CHICKEN

First Meal
A Perfect Roast
  Chicken*
Brandied Pear
  Applesauce*
Baked Butternut
  Squash*
Caesar Salad*

Second Meal
Chicken Tacos* *or*
Avocado Halves
  with Spicy
  Sauce*
Frozen Orange
  Mousse*

Chicken Curry*
Hot rice
Mangoes or papayas

ONE POUND CHICKEN LIVERS

First Meal
Polenta with Chicken
  Livers*
Marinated Vegetables*
Apple Crisp*

Second Meal
Chicken Livers Victoria*
Carrot Parsnip Puree*
Snapdragons*

ONE FLANK STEAK

First Meal
Spicy Stir-Fried Beef*
Fried Rice*
Viennese Apple Soufflé*

Second Meal
Stir-Fried Orange Beef*
Fried Rice*
Stir-Fried Vegetables*

ONE LEG OF LAMB

First Meal
Roast Leg of Lamb*
Broccoli Puree*
Oven-browned
  potatoes
Baked Stuffed
  Apples*

Second Meal
Ground Lamb with
  Feta Cheese and
  Spinach*
Chilled Cucumber
  Soup*

Third Meal
Curried Lamb*
Rice
Mangoes or papayas

12-16 OUNCES FRESH OR FROZEN, SHELLED, DEVEINED SHRIMP

First Meal	*Second Meal*
Shrimp with Feta*	Stir-Fried Shrimp with
Rice	Broccoli*
Spinach and mushroom	Linguine
salad	Sliced tomatoes
Fruit Compote*	Apple Crisp*

SYMBOLS

As you flip through this cookbook you will see one or more symbols beside most of the recipes. These are provided for your ease in finding a dish best suited to the needs of any particular day or week. If you have some extra time on a weekend, for example, there are recipes that can be made ahead and frozen. If you have to have a meal on the table quickly, there are over fifty combinations indicated that can be prepared in less than thirty minutes. Here are brief descriptions of what the eight different symbols mean:

✕   This recipe can be *doubled* easily.

◉   *Versatile*. This recipe can be adapted to different parts of the menu (e.g., appetizer, main dish, or side dish), or to different ingredients (e.g., chicken or turkey).

★   *Quick*. This recipe and the suggested accompaniments (with some freezer backups) can be on the table in under thirty minutes.

‖‖   This recipe is good for using up *leftovers*.

✍   *Seasonal*. This recipe is especially appropriate or possible only during a particular season.

☀   This recipe can be, or is best when, *made ahead*.

■   This recipe can be *frozen*. Reheat in a conventional oven or a microwave oven, where applicable.

❦   *Elegant*.

APPETIZERS

HERBED CHEESE

Use to fill raw mushroom caps, spread on snow peas or in celery sticks, or as a stuffing for chicken breasts.

8 ounces whipped cream cheese, at room temperature
1 tablespoon vegetable oil
1 small clove garlic, finely chopped
3 sprigs parsley, stems removed
1 tablespoon snipped fresh dillweed or ¼ teaspoon dried
2 tablespoons snipped fresh chives or 1 teaspoon freeze-dried
2 to 3 sprigs watercress, stalks removed

1. In a small bowl combine the cheese, oil, and garlic.
2. Chop parsley, chives, and watercress leaves together until fine. Stir into cheese mixture; cover and refrigerate overnight.

SEVICHE and

SOLE-WRAPPED ASPARAGUS

in Fish also make great appetizers

CLAMS OREGANATO
✗ ⊙

An exciting starter for a seafood dinner or double the recipe and serve for luncheon with a salad.

8 round or hard-shelled clams
2 tablespoons butter or margarine, melted
2 tablespoons unflavored fine dry bread crumbs
½ clove garlic, finely chopped
1 tablespoon chopped fresh parsley
2 to 3 drops liquid hot pepper seasoning
½ teaspoon leaf oregano, crumbled

1. Preheat oven or toaster oven to 425 degrees.
2. Scrub clams well and let them soak in salted water with a little cornmeal added if you suspect they are sandy. Drain and rinse and place in a heavy saucepan with ¼ inch of water.
3. Cover pan and steam clams 5 to 8 minutes or until they open. Discard any unopened clams. Remove and discard top shells and place clams, in bottom shells, in baking pan.
4. Combine butter, bread crumbs, garlic, parsley, liquid hot pepper seasoning, and oregano in a small bowl. Spoon over the clams, dividing evenly. Bake 5 minutes; serve immediately (with lemon wedges, if you wish).

CRAB SPREAD

Make ahead and use to fill raw mushrooms, Belgian endive leaves, cherry tomatoes, and snow peas. Or, if you wish, heat in a double boiler and serve on crackers.

1 can (8 ounces) crabmeat, picked over and flaked
4 tablespoons butter, softened
1 tablespoon dark rum
Grated rind of 1 lemon

1. Place crabmeat, butter, and rum in container of electric blender or food processor. Whirl or process until smooth.

2. Add lemon rind and blend briefly. Pack into a small crock or bowl; cover and refrigerate overnight.

POTTED SALMON

✕

The smoked salmon gives a wonderful rich flavor to the spread, but you may use all canned salmon, if you wish. Great to double or quadruple for a party.

¼ pound smoked salmon
4 ounces canned salmon, picked over and flaked
2 tablespoons sweet butter, melted
¼ teaspoon ground cloves
1 flat anchovy fillet or 1 teaspoon anchovy paste
2 teaspoons lemon juice
2 to 3 drops liquid hot pepper seasoning
Pepper

1. Place smoked salmon, canned salmon, butter, cloves, anchovy, lemon juice, liquid hot pepper seasoning, and pepper in the container of an electric blender or food processor and whirl or process until smooth.

2. Pack into a crock or small bowl; cover and refrigerate overnight.

3. Serve on thinly sliced pumpernickel spread with sweet butter and topped with thinly sliced cucumbers.

SHRIMP WITH FENNEL

× ◉

A simple combination that can be made ahead; double the recipe and you'll have a delicious nucleus of a luncheon or dinner salad. Add tomato, cucumber, and radish slices.

4 ounces fresh or frozen, shelled, and deveined shrimp*
1 rib fennel, finely chopped
1 shallot, finely chopped
1 teaspoon lime juice
½ sweet red pepper, cored, seeded and diced
¼ cup Vinaigrette Dressing (page 171)
Boston lettuce leaves
2 lime wedges

1. Plunge the shrimp into a kettle of boiling water and cook 3 to 5 minutes or until shrimp turn pink. Drain; plunge into ice water and drain again.

2. Place shrimp in a medium-size bowl with the fennel, shallot, lime juice, and red pepper. Pour over the dressing; toss to mix; cover and refrigerate 30 minutes or longer.

3. Serve in Boston lettuce cups with lime wedges and a sprig of fennel, if you wish.

* To devein, make a shallow cut down the back of each shrimp and rinse out the vein.

AVOCADO HALVES WITH SPICY SAUCE

✕ ⊙

Serve as an appetizer or as a separate salad course.

2 tablespoons butter or margarine
1 tablespoon water
1 tablespoon tomato catsup
2 to 3 drops liquid hot pepper seasoning
1 tablespoon cider or wine vinegar
1 tablespoon brown sugar
1 teaspoon Worcestershire sauce
1 ripe avocado

1. Combine butter, water, catsup, liquid hot pepper seasoning, vinegar, brown sugar, and Worcestershire sauce in a small saucepan; bring to a boil; simmer 5 minutes, stirring, until well blended and hot.

2. Cut avocado in half and remove pit just before serving.

3. Place avocado halves in small dishes and fill cavities with sauce. Serve with teaspoons.

For a delicious beginning to a

light fish main course, try

OYSTER STEW

in Fish

ROASTED RED PEPPERS WITH ANCHOVIES

X ⊙

Wonderful as is for an appetizer or great as part of an antipasto. I sometimes serve an antipasto with crusty bread as a main dish in the summer or when a light supper is in order.

2 sweet red peppers
1 clove garlic, finely chopped
¼ cup olive oil
1 tablespoon lemon juice
Pepper
6 flat anchovy fillets, chopped

1. Place the peppers on the broiler rack and broil close to the source of heat until they are black on all sides. With tongs or pot holder, transfer peppers to a brown paper bag; close and let stand until cool enough to handle.

2. Peel peppers; core, seed, and cut into strips. Place strips in 2 layers in a flat dish with garlic sprinkled between the layers.

3. Combine oil, lemon juice, pepper, and anchovy fillets and pour over peppers. Cover and refrigerate overnight.

Note: Double or triple the recipe and have on hand to add to salads, meat platters, or chopped to scrambled eggs. Store in a covered container in the refrigerator for up to seven days.

QUICK PIZZA (SPIEDINI)

⊙

Serve this as a snack, first course, or luncheon dish.

2 tablespoons olive oil
1 small clove garlic, finely chopped
2 tablespoons tomato puree or thick tomato sauce
1 tablespoon lemon juice
4 thin slices cooked deli ham, cut in half lengthwise
2 medium-size tomatoes, sliced
6 ounces mozzarella cheese, thinly sliced
2 club or grinder rolls, split

1. In a small saucepan heat the oil and sauté the garlic over low heat for 1 minute.

2. Add the tomato puree and lemon juice and bring to boiling.

3. Arrange the ham, tomato slices, and mozzarella over the split rolls. Spoon the tomato sauce over and broil 6 inches from the source of heat until cheese melts.

REFRIED BEANS

in Sauces, Fillings, and Accompaniments

can be turned into a great appetizer

SOUFFLEED ROULADE WITH MUSHROOM FILLING

◉

Omit the cheese, mustard, salt, pepper, and mushrooms and fill the roll with sliced strawberries and whipped cream for a super dessert for two.

4 tablespoons butter or margarine
2 tablespoons flour
1 cup milk
2 tablespoons freshly grated Parmesan cheese
½ teaspoon Dijon mustard
Salt and pepper
2 eggs, separated
4 medium-size mushrooms, sliced

1. Lightly grease with shortening a 9-inch skillet with a heatproof handle. Line the skillet with wax paper, allowing it to fall over the sides and pressing it down into the skillet. If the skillet does not have a heatproof handle, wrap the handle with aluminum foil.

2. Preheat oven to 375 degrees (a toaster oven is often not big enough). Heat 2 tablespoons of the butter in a medium-size saucepan until melted; stir in the flour and cook, stirring, 1 minute; gradually stir in the milk and bring to a boil, stirring, until mixture is thick and smooth; cook 1 minute.

3. Remove from heat and place half the sauce in a small saucepan. Add cheese to the first mixture and mustard to the second. Season both sauces with salt and pepper.

4. To the cheese mixture, beat in the 2 egg yolks. Beat egg whites until stiff but not dry and stir one-third of the whites into the egg yolk mixture. With a rubber spatula, fold in the remaining egg whites until no streaks of white remain.

5. Turn mixture into prepared skillet; bake 15 minutes. Meanwhile, heat remaining 2 tablespoons butter in a small skillet and sauté mushrooms over high heat 3 to 4 minutes, tossing as they cook.

6. Spray a large napkin or kitchen towel with vegetable spray; turn the baked roulade out onto the sprayed napkin; let stand 2 to 3 minutes; remove paper and, with the help of the napkin, roll up the roulade.

7. Reheat mustard-flavored sauce. Unroll roulade and spread with sautéed mushrooms mixed with 1 tablespoon of the sauce; reroll; cut in half and place each half on a warm plate. Spoon over remaining sauce. Serve immediately.

CRUSTLESS ZUCCHINI QUICHE

Great with a salad for lunch, too.

1 small zucchini
1 tablespoon butter or margarine
2 tablespoons freshly grated Parmesan cheese
½ cup grated Gruyère cheese
2 eggs
¾ cup milk
½ teaspoon Dijon mustard
Pepper

1. Preheat oven or toaster oven to 350 degrees. Trim zucchini and grate on smallest holes or with grater of food processor. Heat butter in a medium-size skillet and sauté the zucchini while stirring, 3 to 4 minutes.

2. Lightly grease a 5-inch pie plate or 2 individual tart pans. Sprinkle the Parmesan over plate or pans; top with zucchini and then Gruyère.

3. In a small bowl mix together the eggs, milk, mustard, and pepper; pour over cheese. Place pie plate or pans on cookie sheet and bake 30 to 35 minutes for plate and 20 to 25 minutes for pans, or until mixture is set. Let stand 5 minutes before serving.

SOUPS

BEAN AND SPINACH SOUP

✕ ⊙ ★

This soup is hearty enough for a main course and is especially nice when followed by a fruit and cheese platter. A meal in 20 minutes.

1 tablespoon vegetable oil
1 medium-size onion, finely chopped
1 clove garlic, finely chopped
1 can (13¾ ounces) chicken broth
1 cup water
2 plum tomatoes, peeled, seeded, and chopped
1 can (20 ounces) cannellini beans, drained and rinsed
½ teaspoon leaf basil, crumbled
½ teaspoon leaf oregano, crumbled
Salt and pepper
½ polybag (10 ounces) fresh spinach, or ½ pound fresh, trimmed, washed, and drained

1. Heat the oil in a medium-size saucepan and sauté the onion and garlic until tender but not browned, about 3 minutes.

2. Add broth, water, tomatoes, beans, basil, oregano, salt and pepper. Bring to a boil; cover and simmer 10 minutes. Add the spinach and reheat to wilt the spinach. Omit adding salt and sprinkle with a little freshly grated Parmesan cheese for an added flavor.

Note: When I use chicken broth in a recipe, I rarely add any additional salt. Learning to reduce the salt in cooking should be a gradual process, and eventually you discover the real flavors of the ingredients.

BROCCOLI SOUP

× ‖‖‖

Great way to use broccoli stalks.

2 tablespoons vegetable oil
1 small onion, finely chopped
1 small clove garlic, finely chopped
Stalks and leaves from 1 bunch broccoli, peeled if tough and
*   diced (about 2 cups)*
1 can (13¾ ounces) chicken broth
Pepper
¼ teaspoon leaf thyme, crumbled

1. In a medium-size saucepan heat the oil and sauté the onion and garlic until tender, about 3 minutes. Add broccoli stalks and leaves and cook, stirring, 3 minutes longer.

2. Add chicken broth, pepper and thyme; bring to a boil. Cover and simmer 25 minutes. Whirl in batches in an electric blender and return to a clean pan. Reheat.

CAULIFLOWER SOUP

A delicate soup to ward off winter's chills when the vegetable is in good supply. Follow with Perfect Roast Chicken (page 53), pan roasted potatoes and oven baked winter squash. Fresh fruit is all you would need for dessert.

1 tablespoon butter or margarine
1 large shallot, finely chopped
2 cups tiny cauliflowerets, about half a small head
1 can (13¾ ounces) chicken broth
½ cup milk
½ cup shredded Gruyère cheese
Pepper

1. Heat the butter in a medium-size saucepan and sauté the shallot until tender but not browned. Add cauliflowerets and cook, stirring, 3 minutes.

2. Add the broth, bring to a boil, cover, and simmer 15 minutes. Pour into the container of an electric blender or food processor and whirl until smooth. Return to clean saucepan; add milk and bring to a boil. Remove from heat and stir in the cheese until melted. Season with pepper. Serve at once.

CREAM OF CELERY AND BLUE CHEESE SOUP

×

This is a rich soup, which is a good first course for a pasta main course such as Linguine with White Clam Sauce (page 180).

3 stalks celery from inside of bunch
½ small onion
1 tablespoon butter
1 cup chicken broth
1 cup light cream or half-and-half
Pepper
2 tablespoons blue cheese, crumbled

1. Chop celery and onion coarsely. Heat butter in a medium-size saucepan and sauté the celery and onion until tender, 2 minutes.
2. Add broth, bring to a boil, cover, and simmer 20 minutes or until celery is soft. Puree in an electric blender or food processor. Return to saucepan; add cream and pepper; reheat.
3. Pour into soup bowls or mugs; add cheese and it will melt as you drink the soup.

RHODE ISLAND CLAM CHOWDER
✕ ⊙

No tomatoes and no milk or cream characterizes the distinctive chowder from the tiny state. Serve it for lunch or before a light fish main course such as Baked Cod with Fresh Tomato Topping (page 31).

2 tablespoons finely chopped lean salt pork or 1 tablespoon
  butter or margarine
1 small onion, finely chopped
1 medium-size potato, cubed
1 pint shucked quahogs (hard clams) or 1 can (10½ ounces)
  minced clams
1 cup water

1. In a medium-size, heavy saucepan sauté the salt pork until the pieces are brown and crispy. Remove with a slotted spoon to paper toweling and reserve. Or, heat the butter.

2. Sauté the onion in the pork fat or butter until tender but not browned. Add potato and cook, stirring, 3 minutes.

3. Drain the clams and add the juice to the saucepan along with the water. Bring to a boil; cover and simmer 15 minutes or until potatoes are tender. Mince the quahogs in a food processor or chop finely with a knife.

4. Add minced clams, return to the boil, and cook 3 to 4 minutes to cook quahogs or serve immediately if using canned clams. Sprinkle with reserved salt pork bits.

CORN CHOWDER
✕

This soup is especially good when local fresh corn is available. Even in the middle of summer there are times when a hot dish is a welcome change, and all you have to add is a salad or light fish dish, such as Pan-Fried Smelts (page 45), or Bay Scallops with Fontina Cheese (page 38). Fresh fruit is the ideal dessert.

1 tablespoon butter or margarine
1 stalk celery, diced
1 medium-size onion, finely chopped
1 can (13¾ ounces) chicken broth or 2 cups water
1 medium-size potato, peeled and diced
Salt and pepper
2 cups corn kernels cut from the cob (about 2 ears) or 1
*   package (10 ounces) frozen corn.*
1 cup milk*

1. Heat the butter in a medium-size saucepan and sauté the celery and onion until tender but not browned, about 4 minutes, stirring frequently.

2. Add broth, potato, salt and pepper. Bring to a boil; cover and simmer 15 minutes or until the potato is tender.

3. Add the corn and milk and bring back to a boil. The corn will be cooked enough as soon as the soup reheats. Serve at once.

Note: As noted in other soup recipes, when I use canned broth, I do not add any salt.

* I let my conscience tell me whether to use whole or skim milk.

CHILLED CUCUMBER SOUP

A soup that needs no cooking and is refreshing on a hot summer day before a main dish salad and raspberries for dessert.

2 medium-size Kirby cucumbers (about 6 ounces each) or
*   12 ounces European-style cucumber, peeled, seeded and*
*   coarsely chopped*
1 small clove garlic, smashed.
1 container (8 ounces) plain yogurt
1 tablespoon snipped fresh dillweed or ½ teaspoon dried
Salt and pepper

Put all the ingredients in the container of an electric blender or food processor and whirl until smooth. Chill.

GAZPACHO

× ★ ✎ ☀

Ready in 10 minutes, this is a refreshing summer soup for any occasion and great to take on a picnic in an insulated container.

½ medium-size cucumber or one large Kirby cucumber
2 plum tomatoes, peeled, seeded and chopped
1 small sweet green pepper, cored, seeded and chopped
1 slice thin white bread, torn into pieces
1 tablespoon red wine vinegar
1 tablespoon olive oil
1 small clove garlic
1 can (12 ounces) vegetable or tomato juice
Salt and pepper
2 scallions with green part, chopped
Tiny garlic croutons

1. Peel, seed, and coarsely chop the cucumber and place in the container of an electric blender or food procesor. Add the tomatoes, pepper, bread, vinegar, oil, garlic, and juice.

2. Whirl until smooth. Taste and add salt and pepper to taste. I find the canned juice adds enough salt for my taste. Chill well.

3. Serve in chilled bowls sprinkled with scallions and croutons.

LENTIL SOUP

X ⦿ ■

A hearty soup that is great for lunch or teamed with a main dish salad such as Ham and Lima Bean Salad (page 160) or a light main dish such as French Pizza (page 120), makes a fine meal winter or summer. The recipe can be doubled or quadrupled for freezing in meal-size portions.

> 2 tablespoons vegetable oil
> 1 small onion, finely chopped
> 1 small clove garlic, finely chopped
> 1 carrot, diced
> 1 large stalk celery, diced
> Few celery leaves if available, chopped
> ¼ cup lentils, picked over and washed
> 1 can (13¾ ounces) chicken broth
> Pepper
> ⅛ teaspoon leaf thyme, crumbled
> 1 cup chopped escarole, kale, chard or spinach
> 1 tablespoon chopped fresh parsley

1. Heat the oil in a heavy kettle or Dutch oven and sauté the onion over low heat for 5 minutes. Add the garlic, carrot, celery, and celery leaves and sauté 3 minutes longer.

2. Add lentils, chicken broth, pepper to taste, and thyme; bring to a boil; cover and simmer 40 minutes or until lentils are tender.

3. Add escarole or other green and cook 1 minute; add parsley and serve.

MUSHROOM SOUP

×

Serve as a luncheon accompaniment to a favorite sandwich or as a first course for a light main dish such as sautéed turkey cutlets with pureed fresh peas.

2 tablespoons vegetable oil
1 medium-size onion, finely chopped
1 stalk celery with leaves, diced
1 carrot, diced
8 ounces mushrooms, sliced
1 can (13¾ ounces) chicken broth or 2 cups water
½ teaspoon leaf rosemary, crumbled
Salt and pepper
1 tablespoon chopped fresh parsley

1. Heat 1 tablespoon of the oil in a heavy saucepan and sauté the onion until tender but not browned, about 3 minutes.

2. Add celery and carrot and cook, stirring often, 2 minutes. Add remaining oil and mushrooms and sauté 3 minutes longer, stirring often. Add broth, rosemary, salt and pepper; bring to a boil; cover and simmer 10 minutes. Sprinkle with parsley and serve.

Note: When I use canned broth, I do not add any salt.

FRENCH ONION SOUP

✕ ⊙

Wonderful beginning to any meal and a super luncheon special.

1 tablespoon butter
1 large sweet onion, thinly sliced
2 teaspoons sugar
1 can (13¾ ounces) beef or chicken broth
Pepper
Pinch leaf thyme, crumbled
4 slices (¼ inch thick) French bread or club roll
½ cup grated Jarlsberg or Fontina cheese

1. Melt the butter in a medium-size heavy saucepan; add the onion, cover, and cook over medium heat 10 minutes or until onion is tender. Sprinkle with sugar and cook, stirring often, until sugar caramelizes.

2. Add broth, pepper to taste, and thyme; bring to a boil; cover and simmer 15 minutes. Preheat oven or toaster oven to 450 degrees.

3. Meanwhile, toast the bread slices. Place 2 toasted bread slices in each of two heatproof ramekins or French onion soup bowls. Pour over the soup, sprinkle with the cheese, and bake in preheated 450-degree oven until the cheese is melted and browned.

SPLIT PEA SOUP

✕ ⊙

In less than an hour you can fix this soup to enjoy with crusty bread, a tossed green salad and a dessert such as Frozen Chocolate Dessert from the freezer (page 208).

1 tablespoon butter or margarine
1 medium-size onion, finely chopped
1 carrot, diced
1 stalk celery, diced with leaves
1 can (13¾ ounces) chicken broth or 2 cups water
1 cup water
½ cup green or yellow split peas, picked over and washed
Salt and pepper
¼ teaspoon leaf thyme, crumbled
½ bay leaf, crumbled

1. In a medium-size saucepan heat the butter and sauté the onion until tender but not browned, about 4 minutes.

2. Add the carrot and celery and cook, stirring occasionally, until barely tender, about 5 minutes. Add broth, water, split peas, salt, pepper, thyme, and bay leaf.

3. Bring to a boil; cover and simmer 45 minutes or until split peas are tender. Blend in about three batches in an electric blender or food processor and return to a clean saucepan. Reheat.

Note: I do not add salt when using chicken broth.

POTATO AND LEEK SOUP

×

Great beginning for any meal, summer or winter.

2 medium-size leeks, trimmed and washed well, halved lengthwise and sliced into ⅛-inch pieces
2 tablespoons butter or margarine
1 medium-size potato, pared and diced
1 can (13¾ ounces) chicken broth
Pepper to taste
1 cup water
½ cup light or heavy cream

1. In a medium-size saucepan sauté the leeks in the butter until tender, about 5 minutes, stirring often. Add the potato and sauté 3 minutes longer, stirring often.

2. Add the chicken broth, pepper, and water. Bring to a boil; cover and simmer 25 minutes or until potatoes are tender.

3. Whirl the soup in two batches in an electric blender or food processor and return to a clean pan. To serve hot, add cream and reheat but do not boil. To serve cold, refrigerate the pureed mixture. Add the cream just before serving.

Note: Use the other 2 leeks in the bunch in Braised Leeks (page 138).

MR. CORNWALL'S TOMATO COBB
✕ ✍

For the summer's best cold soup, make this with the finest ripest tomatoes from the garden or fruit stand.

3 large ripe tomatoes
2 tablespoons grated onion
Salt and pepper
2 tablespoons mayonnaise
½ teaspoon curry powder or to taste

1. Peel tomatoes by dipping into boiling water for a count of seven. Remove and plunge into ice water. Peel, halve, seed, and finely chop.

2. In a bowl combine chopped tomatoes, onion, salt and pepper. Chill several hours. Serve with a tablespoon of mayonnaise mixed with the curry powder. Just before eating, swirl the mayonnaise into the soup.

ZUCCHINI SOUP
✕ ◉ ★

A simple, easy-to-make soup that is good hot or cold. In summer, team it with a main dish salad and in colder weather with a light Chicken Breasts Parmesan (page 68), and sugar snap peas. Either way, dinner is ready in less than 30 minutes.

1 tablespoon vegetable oil
1 medium-size onion, finely chopped
1 small clove garlic, finely chopped
2 small (4 ounces each) zucchini, sliced
1 can (13¾ ounces) chicken broth or 2 cups water
2 teaspoons snipped fresh dillweed or ¼ teaspoon dried
Salt and pepper
¼ cup plain yogurt, if serving cold

1. Heat the oil in a heavy saucepan and sauté the onion and garlic until tender but not browned, about 3 minutes.

2. Add the zucchini and sauté 3 minutes, stirring often. Add the broth, dill, and pepper; bring to a boil; cover and simmer 15 minutes.

3. Place in the container of an electric blender or food processor and whirl until smooth. To avoid overflow in a blender, start running at low speed and gradually increase to highest speed.

4. If you wish to serve hot, return blended mixture to a clean pan and reheat; to serve cold, chill well, and whisk in the yogurt just before serving.

FISH

BAKED COD WITH FRESH TOMATO TOPPING

For dinner in less than 30 minutes, serve with green beans, boiled new potatoes, tossed green salad, and fresh fruit.

1 tablespoon vegetable oil
1 small shallot or scallion, chopped
½ small clove garlic, finely chopped
6 plum tomatoes, skinned and chopped
1 tablespoon chopped fresh basil or ½ teaspoon leaf, crumbled
Salt and pepper
1 pound cod fillet, cut in half crosswise
2 tablespoons butter or margarine
2 tablespoons lemon juice

1. Preheat oven or toaster oven to 375 degrees.

2. Heat the oil in a small saucepan and sauté the shallot and garlic until tender but not browned. Add tomatoes, basil, salt, and pepper and bring to a boil. Simmer, uncovered, 2 minutes.

3. Meanwhile, arrange the cod in a buttered shallow baking dish or 2 individual au gratin dishes. Dot with butter, sprinkle with lemon juice, and spoon the tomato sauce over the fillets.

4. Bake for 15 minutes or until the fish is opaque and flakes easily.

HADDOCK WITH DILL BUTTER

Serve with boiled new potatoes and Broccoli Puree (page 133), and fresh pineapple for dinner in less than 30 minutes.

2 tablespoons butter or margarine
1 small shallot, finely chopped
2 tablespoons lemon juice
2 tablespoons snipped fresh dillweed*
Salt and pepper
1 pound fillet haddock, cut in half crosswise

1. Preheat oven or toaster oven to 375 degrees.
2. Heat the butter in a small saucepan and sauté the shallot until tender but not browned. Add the lemon juice, dill, salt, and pepper.
3. Arrange the haddock in a buttered shallow baking dish or 2 individual au gratin dishes. Pour the dill sauce over and bake for 15 minutes or until fish is opaque and flakes easily.

* If fresh dill is not available, substitute a mixture of fresh chopped parsley and chives.

FINNAN HADDIE DUGLERÉ

Dugleré means tomatoes; finnan haddie is smoked haddock. Serve with rice, mixed green salad, and made-ahead Maple Rum Custard (page 208) for dessert.

1 shallot, finely chopped
12 ounces finnan haddie
Dry white wine or vermouth
2 sprigs fresh parsley
1 sprig fresh thyme or ½ teaspoon leaf, crumbled
1 large ripe tomato, peeled, seeded and chopped or ¾ cup
 canned plum tomatoes, drained and chopped
Pepper

1. Preheat oven or toaster oven to 350 degrees. Sprinkle shallot over bottom of a buttered small baking dish just big enough to hold the fish.

2. Place fish on top of shallot; pour in wine to come halfway up the fish. Add parsley and thyme. Cover baking dish with foil.

3. Bake 25 minutes or until fish flakes easily. Remove fish to cool slightly.

4. Discard sprigs of herbs. Pour liquid and shallot into a medium-size skillet. Add tomato, bring to a boil, and cook until slightly thickened. Flake the fish and add to the sauce. Season with pepper.

KEDGEREE
◉ |||||

An unusual brunch, lunch, or supper dish that uses up leftover cooked fish and rice. Serve with chutney and corn fritters.

1 cup cooked firm fish, such as cod, haddock, bass, sole, scrod, or finnan haddie, flaked
1 cup cooked rice
2 hard-cooked eggs, whites and yolks separated and chopped
¼ cup milk or heavy cream
½ teaspoon curry powder
Salt and pepper
1 tablespoon chopped fresh parsley

1. Preheat oven or toaster oven to 350 degrees.

2. In a medium-size bowl combine fish, rice and chopped egg whites. Mix milk with the curry powder and stir into fish mixture. Season with salt and pepper.

3. Turn into a small buttered baking dish and bake 20 minutes or until hot through. Sprinkle with chopped parsley mixed with chopped egg yolks.

MUSSELS IN WHITE WINE

It takes more time to clean mussels than to cook them. For dinner in less than 30 minutes, serve with French bread for mopping up juices, mixed green salad, and Flambéed Bananas (page 200) for dessert.

2 quarts fresh mussels
½ medium onion, finely chopped
¼ cup chopped fresh parsley
Sprig of fresh thyme or ¼ teaspoon leaf, crumbled
4 tablespoons butter
Pepper
1 cup dry white wine

1. To clean mussels, scrape off any barnacles and dirt using a sharp paring knife and working under cold running water. With your fingers, pull back the beard and yank it off; brush well. Put cleaned mussels in a bowl of cold salted water.

2. In a large kettle or saucepan put the onion, 2 tablespoons of the parsley, and 2 tablespoons of the butter.

3. Add the drained mussels to the kettle; sprinkle lightly with pepper and pour in the wine.

4. Set over high heat, partially covered. When liquid begins to boil, turn down the heat and cook 5 to 10 minutes or until mussels have opened. Discard any that remain closed. Scoop into soup plates; add remaining butter and parsley to kettle; bring to a boil and pour over mussels.

OYSTER STEW

⊙ ★

Just right for a light lunch or supper or as a beginning to a light fish main course. Serve with oyster crackers and a dry white wine.

1 pint fresh oysters
1 cup milk
1 cup light cream
1 teaspoon Worcestershire sauce
2 tablespoons butter
Pepper
Paprika

1. Pick over the oysters for bits of shell; strain and put liquor in a medium-size saucepan; bring to a boil. Add the oysters and cook just until the edges curl, about 1 minute.

2. Heat the milk and cream together in a small saucepan. Add to oysters with Worcestershire sauce. Reheat but do not boil. Whirl in the butter and pepper to taste.

3. Pour into hot soup bowls and sprinkle with paprika, if you wish.

For a delicious luncheon dish, see

CLAMS OREGANATO

in Appetizers

DILLED SALMON STEAKS

For dinner in less than 30 minutes, serve with Zucchini Limone (page 150), boiled new potatoes, and fresh fruit for dessert.

1½ tablespoons butter or margarine
1 small shallot, finely chopped
3 tablespoons lemon juice
2 teaspoons country-style Dijon mustard
2 tablespoons snipped fresh dillweed*
Salt and pepper
2 salmon steaks, about 8 to 12 ounces each

1. Heat the butter in a small saucepan and sauté the shallot until tender but not browned. Add lemon juice, mustard, dill, salt, and pepper. Bring to a boil, stirring. Preheat oven or toaster oven to 375 degrees.

2. Place the salmon steaks in a buttered shallow baking dish or in individual au gratin dishes.

3. Pour the sauce over the steaks and bake for 25 minutes or until fish is opaque and flakes easily.

* I would not make this dish unless I had fresh dill.

SCALLOPS IN WHITE WINE

For a meal in less than 30 minutes, serve with sautéed julienned zucchini and yellow squash, French bread, mixed green salad, and Frozen Orange Mousse (page 202), made ahead and stored in the freezer.

12 ounces bay scallops or sea scallops, quartered
1 teaspoon lemon juice
2 tablespoons dry white wine or vermouth
1 tablespoon snipped fresh chives
1 tablespoon chopped fresh parsley
1 teaspoon snipped fresh dillweed
Pepper
¼ cup heavy cream or dry white wine
2 tablespoons soft bread crumbs
1 tablespoon freshly grated Parmesan cheese
1 tablespoon butter or margarine

1. Preheat oven or toaster oven to 450 degrees. Rinse and dry scallops and place in small, shallow, buttered baking dish, 2 ramekins, or individual au gratin dishes.

2. Combine the lemon juice, wine, chives, parsley, dillweed and pepper and pour over scallops. Toss to coat. Pour cream over.

3. Combine crumbs and Parmesan cheese; sprinkle over scallops. Dot with butter. Bake 10 minutes and glaze under the broiler.

BAY SCALLOPS WITH FONTINA CHEESE

For dinner in less than 30 minutes, serve with Confetti Rice (page 177), Cole Slaw with Peppers and Pickles (page 162), and fruit sherbet for dessert.

8 to 12 ounces bay scallops
2 tablespoons lemon juice
4 tablespoons dry vermouth
2 tablespoons soft bread crumbs
4 tablespoons finely grated Fontina cheese

1. Preheat oven or toaster oven to 425 degrees.
2. Rinse and dry the scallops and place in a shallow, buttered baking dish or 2 individual au gratin dishes.
3. Pour the lemon juice and vermouth over the scallops. Mix the bread crumbs with the cheese and sprinkle over the scallops. Bake for 15 minutes or until scallops are cooked and cheese has melted.

LINGUINE WITH SCALLOP SAUCE

For dinner in less than 30 minutes, serve with crusty bread, a tossed green salad, and Peach Syllabub (page 203).

1 tablespoon vegetable oil
2 small shallots, finely chopped
2 cups Well-Seasoned Tomato Sauce (page 187)
12 ounces bay scallops, rinsed and dried
1 tablespoon chopped fresh parsley
8 ounces linguine
Freshly grated Parmesan cheese

1. In a medium-size skillet heat the oil and sauté the shallots until tender but not browned.
2. Add the sauce; bring to a boil; add the scallops and simmer 3 minutes. Meanwhile, cook the linguine according to label directions to the *al dente* stage; drain.

3. Divide pasta between two warm plates and top with scallop sauce; sprinkle with Parmesan cheese. Pass extra cheese, if you wish.

SCALLOPS FLORENTINE

Dinner can be ready in less than 30 minutes if you serve this delicate dish with Lemon Rice (page 178) and Buttered Pears in Cream (page 204).

1 bag (10 ounces) washed spinach or 1 pound fresh, trimmed, or 1 package (10 ounces) frozen chopped spinach
3 ounces cream cheese, softened
Pinch ground nutmeg
Salt and pepper
8 to 12 ounces bay scallops, rinsed and dried
2 tablespoons butter or margarine
2 tablespoons lemon juice

1. Wash and drain the fresh spinach and cook in the water clinging to the leaves until wilted. Cook frozen spinach according to label directions. Drain and press out excess liquid from spinach. Preheat oven or toaster oven to 425 degrees.

2. Place spinach in a bowl. Beat in the cream cheese, nutmeg, salt, and pepper. Divide the mixture between two buttered, individual au gratin dishes; top with scallops, dividing equally.

3. Dot with butter and sprinkle with lemon juice. Cover tightly with aluminum foil and bake for 15 minutes. Serve at once.

FRIED BAY SCALLOPS

For a meal in less than 30 minutes, serve with Blender Mushroom Sauce (page 188), Stir-Fried Asparagus and Snow Peas (page 130), sliced tomato salad, and Flambéed Bananas (page 200).

8 to 12 ounces bay scallops
1 egg, lightly beaten
1½ cups plain dry bread crumbs or white cornmeal
Salt and pepper
Vegetable oil for frying

1. Rinse and dry the scallops. A few at a time, coat with egg and then roll in the crumbs mixed with salt and pepper. Set, not touching, on wax paper to dry for 10 to 20 minutes.

2. Pour oil into a large heavy skillet to a depth of ¼ inch. Heat to 360 degrees on a deep-fat thermometer or hot enough to brown a cube of bread in 1 minute.

3. Fry the scallops in about three batches so that the temperature of the oil does not drop dramatically. Fry 1 to 2 minutes or until browned on all sides. Do not overcook. Drain on paper toweling and keep warm until all are fried.

SEVICHE

Serve as a first course or a luncheon dish with croissants, mixed green salad, sherbet and fresh fruit.

½ pound fresh bay or sea scallops, quartered
⅓ cup fresh lime juice
2 tablespoons vegetable oil
1 tablespoon finely chopped onion
3 tablespoons chopped fresh parsley
1 small clove garlic, finely chopped
1 tablespoon canned chopped green chilies
2 to 3 drops liquid hot pepper seasoning
Salt and pepper

1. In a glass or ceramic bowl combine scallops, lime juice, oil, onion, parsley, garlic, chilies, hot pepper seasoning, salt and pepper. Refrigerate at least 4 hours.

2. Serve in ramekins or scallop shells.

Note: Do not attempt this dish with anything but the freshest of scallops. The lime juice "cooks" them.

SHRIMP WITH FETA

Serve with plain rice and a big spinach salad. Splurge and buy a couple of pieces of baklava at the local Greek pastry shop, for dessert.

1 tablespoon olive oil
1 small onion, finely chopped
1 small clove garlic, finely chopped
2 cups tomato puree
¼ teaspoon leaf basil, crumbled
⅛ teaspoon fennel seeds
Salt and pepper
2 tablespoons chopped fresh parsley
6 ounces fresh or frozen, shelled and deveined shrimp
⅓ cup crumbled feta cheese

1. Heat the oil in a medium-size skillet and sauté the onion and garlic until tender, about 2 minutes.

2. Stir in the puree, basil, fennel, salt, and pepper. Bring to a boil, stirring. Cover and simmer 10 minutes.

3. Add the parsley and shrimp and cook just until shrimp have turned pink, about 5 minutes. Add the feta and stir to mix.

Note: Having a 12-ounce bag of frozen, shelled and deveined shrimp in the freezer encourages you to make this dish and maybe the following recipe, Stir-Fried Shrimp with Broccoli, another day.

STIR-FRIED SHRIMP WITH BROCCOLI

Serve with Fried Rice (page 175) or plain rice and dried fruit compote and cookies for dessert.

6 ounces fresh or frozen, shelled and deveined shrimp
2 tablespoons vegetable oil
2 teaspoons chopped fresh ginger root
1 clove garlic, finely chopped
½ cup diced celery
½ can (8 ounces) water chestnuts, sliced, or bamboo shoots
2 cups broccoli flowerets
⅓ cup clam or chicken broth
1 tablespoon dry sherry
1 tablespoon soy sauce
1 teaspoon cornstarch

1. In a wok or heavy skillet stir-fry the shrimp in 1 tablespoon of the oil until pink, about 4 minutes. Remove by slotted spoon to a bowl.

2. Add the remaining tablespoon of oil to the skillet and stir-fry the ginger, garlic, and celery for 2 minutes.

3. Add the water chestnuts and broccoli and stir-fry 2 minutes, adding more oil if needed. Return shrimp to wok.

4. In a 1-cup measure, mix the broth, sherry, soy sauce, and cornstarch until smooth. Pour over shrimp and vegetables and cook, stirring, until sauce thickens and coats.

Note: Use broccoli stalks for Broccoli Soup (page 16) and remaining flowerets in salad, as crudités or steam for a vegetable.

CREAMY SHRIMP CURRY

Serve the curry over rice with a choice of peanuts, chutney, chopped scallion, raisins, sliced bananas, and chopped candied ginger. Serve with Marinated Vegetables (page 169) or cucumbers in yogurt. Fresh pineapple is great for dessert and you will have enough left for another day. Quarter the fruit lengthwise and loosen flesh, remove core, cut into triangles, and serve outrigger-style.

2 tablespoons vegetable oil
1 small onion, finely chopped
½ tart apple, cored and finely chopped
1 tablespoon flour
2 teaspoons curry powder or to taste
¼ teaspoon ground ginger
Salt
1 cup clam or chicken broth
½ pound fresh shrimp or 6 ounces frozen, shelled and deveined
1 tablespoon lime or lemon juice
3 tablespoons heavy cream or milk

1. Heat the oil in a heavy skillet. Sauté the onion and apple until tender, about 2 minutes.

2. Sprinkle over the flour, curry powder, ginger, and salt to taste. Cook, stirring, 2 minutes. Gradually stir in the broth; bring to a boil, stirring, until sauce is thick and smooth. Simmer 20 minutes.

3. Shell and devein shrimp if fresh. Add shrimp and lime juice to skillet and cook 3 to 4 minutes until shrimp are pink and firm. Stir in cream; reheat but to not boil.

Note: Double or quadruple the recipe without the shrimp and cream and freeze in boilable bags in meal-size portions. If the sauce is made with chicken broth it can be the base for both shrimp and chicken curries. For each recipe of sauce, add 1½ to 2 cups cooked diced chicken or turkey.

STIR-FRIED SHRIMP WITH PEPPERS

Serve with Fried Rice (page 175) or plain rice and Frozen Chocolate Dessert (page 208) for dinner in less than 30 minutes.

6 ounces fresh or frozen, shelled and deveined shrimp
2 tablespoons vegetable oil
1 tablespoon chopped fresh ginger root
2 scallions, cut into 2-inch lengths on the bias
2 small sweet green peppers, cored, seeded, and sliced
½ can (8 ounces) water chestnuts (7 to 8), sliced
1½ tablespoons dry sherry
1½ tablespoons soy sauce
1 teaspoon cornstarch
2 tablespoons water
¼ teaspoon hot red pepper flakes, or to taste

1. In a wok or heavy skillet stir-fry the shrimp in 1 tablespoon of the oil until pink, about 4 minutes.

2. Remove shrimp with a slotted spoon to a bowl. Add the remaining oil to the wok and stir-fry the ginger, scallions, and peppers for 3 minutes.

3. Return the shrimp to the wok. Mix together the sherry, soy sauce, cornstarch, and water until smooth. Stir into shrimp mixture with hot pepper flakes and cook, stirring, until sauce thickens and coats.

Note: Leftover water chestnuts can go into Stir-Fried Shrimp with Broccoli (page 42) or into a spinach salad.

PAN-FRIED SMELTS

These little fish make a great meal for two in less than 30 minutes if you serve them with Stir-Fried Asparagus and Snow Peas (page 130), crusty bread, sliced tomato salad, and Apple Almond Tarts (page 197) from the freezer.

1 pound cleaned smelts
¼ cup flour or white cornmeal
Pepper
Vegetable oil for frying
Lemon wedges

1. Wash and dry the smelts; season the flour or cornmeal with pepper and place in a plastic bag. Dredge the smelts in the flour mixture a few at a time.

2. In a heavy skillet pour oil to a depth of ¼ inch and heat. Fry the smelts a few at a time so they do not touch each other, for 2 minutes on a side; drain on paper towel and keep warm until all are cooked. Serve with lemon wedges.

SOLE IN CHAMPAGNE SAUCE

There may be a time when you have leftover champagne, or you can buy a split, or, better yet, buy a bottle and drink the rest with the meal. For dinner in less than 30 minutes, serve with carrot puree, Zucchini Limone (page 150), mixed green salad, and Russian Raspberries (page 205) for dessert.

2 tablespoons diced carrot (½ medium)
½ small onion, finely chopped
2 sole fillets, about 4 to 6 ounces each
¾ cup champagne
Salt and pepper
1 tablespoon butter, softened
1 tablespoon flour
3 tablespoons heavy cream or champagne
¼ cup peeled seeded green grapes

1. Preheat oven or toaster oven to 350 degrees.

2. Scatter carrot and onion over bottom of small buttered baking dish. Roll up fillets, skin side in, and set them seam side down on vegetables. Pour champagne over; season with salt and pepper. Cover dish tightly and bake for 20 to 25 minutes or until fish is opaque through.

3. With a slotted spoon, remove fillets to a warm platter and keep warm. Make a paste by mixing the butter and flour together; pour liquid from baking dish into a small saucepan; set over medium heat and bring to a boil. Gradually whisk in the butter and flour mixture until sauce is smooth and thickened. Stir in the cream and reheat. Pour over fillets and garnish with grapes.

Note: Four small flounder fillets can be substituted for the sole and white wine for the champagne.

SOLE KIEV

A variation on a theme, which does not have to be deep fried. Serve with red-skinned new potatoes, Summer Garden Peas (page 143), Boston or Bibb lettuce salad, and Mocha Mousse (page 209) made ahead and stored in the freezer. Dinner is ready in less than 30 minutes.

2 sole fillets, about 6 ounces each
4 raw shrimp, shelled, deveined and finely chopped
2 tablespoons butter or margarine, softened
⅛ teaspoon ground nutmeg
1 teaspoon snipped fresh dillweed, or ¼ teaspoon dried
1 tablespoon chopped fresh parsley
2 drops liquid hot pepper seasoning
1 tablespoon lemon juice
1 egg, lightly beaten
2 teaspoons cold water
¼ cup fine, unflavored dry bread crumbs
2 tablespoons butter, melted
1 slice lemon, cut in half and dipped in chopped parsley

1. Place fish fillets between sheets of wax paper. Pound with a mallet, rolling pin, or heavy pan until thin enough to roll.

2. Combine shrimp, softened butter, nutmeg, dill, parsley, hot pepper seasoning, and lemon juice. Mix well; spread over fillets; roll up from the long side, tucking in the edges as you roll.

3. In a saucer mix the egg and water. Spread crumbs on wax paper. Coat rolls in egg and then in crumbs, repeating if necessary to get a good coating. Chill 30 minutes.

4. Preheat oven or toaster oven to 450 degrees. Place fish rolls in small buttered baking dish; pour over melted butter. Bake for 10 minutes or until fish is opaque through. Garnish with lemon slices.

Note: Substitute large flounder fillets for the sole, if you wish.

SOLE-WRAPPED ASPARAGUS
⊙ ★

Serve one bundle for an appetizer or two bundles for a main dish. For dinner in less than 30 minutes, serve with Lima Beans in Cream and Chives (page 139), Boston lettuce salad, and fresh fruit for dessert.

12 stalks of medium-thick asparagus
4 sole or flounder fillets (3 to 4 ounces each)
2 tablespoons oil
2 tablespoons vermouth
Salt and pepper
1 slice bread
¾ cup chicken broth
½ cup walnuts
½ teaspoon paprika
1 teaspoon horseradish, drained, or to taste

1. Snap asparagus stalks where they break naturally and wash well. Lay spears flat in a skillet and pour boiling water to cover. Cover pan and cook 5 to 6 minutes or until crisp tender. Drain in colander and then on paper towel. Preheat oven or toaster oven to 400 degrees.

2. Wrap 3 stalks asparagus in each sole or flounder fillet. Place in one layer in a shallow baking dish. Pour over oil and vermouth; sprinkle with salt and pepper. Cover and bake 10 minutes or until fish is opaque. Remove fish to a warm platter.

3. Combine bread, 2 tablespoons broth and walnuts in container of an electric blender or food processor. Whirl until smooth.

4. Add paprika and remaining broth gradually until mixture is consistency of thin mayonnaise; blend in horseradish. Spread over fillets and serve immediately.

STUFFED SOLE
× ★

For dinner in 30 minutes, serve with spinach puree, skillet fried potatoes, Endive and Beet Salad (page 163), and Fruit Compote (page 207) for dessert.

1 tablespoon butter
1 shallot or scallion, finely chopped
2 ounces mushrooms, sliced
1 teaspoon lemon juice
1 tablespoon chopped fresh parsley
¼ cup soft bread crumbs*
Salt and pepper
2 sole fillets (3 to 4 ounces each)†
2 teaspoons butter

1. Melt the tablespoon of butter in a small heavy skillet and sauté the shallot until tender, about 3 minutes.

2. Add mushrooms and lemon juice and cook, stirring, 3 minutes. Add parsley, bread crumbs, salt, and pepper. Mix well.

3. Preheat oven or toaster oven to 375 degrees. Butter a small baking dish.

4. Lay fillets, skin side up, on board. Divide mushroom mixture between fillets. Roll up and place, seam side down, in baking dish. Dot fish with remaining 2 teaspoons butter. Bake 15 to 20 minutes or until fish is opaque through.

* I use sourdough bread crumbs when possible.

† Four small flounder fillets can be substituted for the sole.

BUTTERFLIED AND STUFFED SWORDFISH

Serve with home fries and frenched green beans, cole slaw, and fruit pie for dessert.

1 pound fresh swordfish in one steak
1 tablespoon vegetable oil
1 shallot, finely chopped
½ ripe tomato, peeled, seeded and chopped
1 hard-cooked egg yolk, chopped
1 tablespoon snipped fresh dillweed or chopped fresh parsley
2 tablespoons soft bread crumbs
Salt and pepper
2 tablespoons butter, softened
½ cup unflavored dry bread crumbs

1. With a long sharp knife, slice through swordfish horizontally to the edge of the skin and open it up like a butterfly.

2. Heat the oil in a small skillet and sauté the shallot 2 minutes. Add tomato and cook over medium heat until mixture thickens. Add egg yolk, dill, soft bread crumbs, salt, and pepper. Spread the mixture inside the fish; press back together to form one steak. Preheat broiler.

3. Spread both sides of fish with butter and coat with crumbs. Place fish on broiler rack 6 to 8 inches from preheated broiler. Broil 10 minutes on each side; test if fish is opaque through; if not, bake in a preheated 350-degree oven or toaster oven 5 to 8 minutes longer.

POULTRY

A PERFECT ROAST CHICKEN

When you have 1½ hours to fix dinner, the bonus is leftovers for another day. Serve half of the chicken with Brandied Pear Apple Sauce (page 189), roasted potatoes, Baked Butternut Squash (page 148), mixed green salad, and cheese and fruit for dessert. The other half of the bird can be used in hash, salad, Hot Chicken Mousse (page 73), or Chicken Pot Pies (page 70).

1 roasting chicken, about 4 pounds
Salt and pepper
½ lemon
1 small bunch fresh tarragon, rosemary, thyme, sage, or
  parsley
2 tablespoons butter or margarine, softened.

1. Preheat oven to 375 degrees.

2. Remove extra fat from cavity of chicken; sprinkle with salt and pepper and rub with cut lemon.

3. Cut lemon into quarters and put in the cavity with the herb. Spread butter over breast and legs. Place chicken on its side on a rack in a roasting pan. Roast 25 minutes, basting twice.

4. Turn chicken on its other side and roast 25 minutes more, basting twice. Turn chicken breast side up; baste and roast for 20 minutes. Chicken is done when leg joint moves easily and juices run clear.

Note: In line with today's lighter eating patterns, I do not make a gravy or sauce.

ROAST CORNISH GAME HEN

Since Cornish hens have been available fresh as well as frozen, they make a very convenient and quick meal for two. I find a large hen (1¾ pounds) ample for two, but you need two at 12 ounces each. In the spring, I serve asparagus, citrus salad and Baked Stuffed Apples (page 200). In winter, creamed spinach or steamed broccoli is the choice for a vegetable.

1 Rock Cornish game hen (about 1¾ pounds), thawed if
frozen
2 tablespoons butter
1 small onion, finely chopped
1 stalk celery, finely diced
¾ cup soft bread crumbs
Salt and pepper
1½ tablespoons chopped fresh parsley
½ teaspoon leaf rosemary, crumbled
2 tablespoons lemon juice
2 tablespoons butter, melted
½ teaspoon cornstarch

1. Remove giblets and place in a small saucepan with 1 cup water; bring to a boil; cover and simmer while bird is roasting. Preheat oven or toaster oven to 375 degrees.

2. Rinse and dry the hen inside and out. Heat 2 tablespoons butter in a small skillet and sauté the onion and celery until tender, about 3 minutes.

3. Add bread crumbs, salt, pepper, parsley, rosemary, and lemon juice to the skillet. Mix well and use to stuff the hen. Place in a small baking dish and roast for 1¼ hours, basting several times with the melted butter, or until no pink juices escape when thigh is pricked.

4. Remove giblets and discard. Boil the broth rapidly until volume is reduced to ½ cup. Mix ½ teaspoon cornstarch with 2 tablespoons cold water until smooth. Stir into boiling broth and cook 1 minute. Season with salt and pepper. Serve separately.

CORNISH GAME HENS IN PORT WINE

This can be an elegant meal, ready in less than an hour, with no leftovers if you buy small hens. Serve with Wild Rice (page 178), or brown rice, stir-fried broccoli with sesame seeds, marinated Mushroom Salad (page 164) and strawberries Romanoff for dessert.

Cornish game hens, about ¾ pound each, thawed if frozen.
Salt and pepper
½ teaspoon leaf thyme, crumbled
1 small tart apple, halved and cored
1 small onion, halved
2 tablespoons butter or margarine
1 tablespoon vegetable oil
⅔ cup apple cider or apple juice
⅓ cup port wine
3 tablespoons ginger marmalade or bitter orange marmalade
¼ cup golden raisins
1 tablespoon cornstarch
1 tablespoon cold water

1. Preheat oven or toaster oven to 350 degrees.

2. Sprinkle cavities of hens with salt, pepper, and thyme. Place half an apple and half an onion in each cavity.

3. Heat the butter and oil in a heavy Dutch oven or casserole. Brown the birds on all sides in the butter mixture.

4. In a small saucepan combine the cider, port, and marmalade; heat, stirring, until blended. Pour over birds; cover dish tightly and bake 50 minutes or until legs move easily and clear juices flow when legs are pricked.

5. Remove birds to a heated platter and keep warm. Add raisins to casserole and bring to a boil. Mix cornstarch with the water until smooth; stir into sauce and cook, stirring, until thickened and clear. Pour sauce over birds or serve separately.

APRICOT AND RICE STUFFED
CORNISH GAME HENS

Serve with Wilted Spinach (page 147), Endive and Beet Salad (page 163), and fresh fruit for dessert.

2 tablespoons butter or margarine
1 small onion, finely chopped
1½ cups cooked rice, about ½ cup raw, cooked according to label directions
1 dozen dried apricots, chopped (½ cup)
Salt and pepper
2 tablespoons pignolia nuts
2 Cornish game hens (about ¾ pound each), thawed if frozen
¼ cup apricot preserves
1 tablespoon finely chopped fresh ginger root

1. Preheat oven or toaster oven to 350 degrees.

2. Heat the butter in a small skillet and sauté the onion until tender. Place the rice in a medium-size bowl; add the onion mixture, apricots, salt, pepper, and nuts. Mix well.

3. Use rice mixture to stuff the birds that have been washed, dried, and seasoned if you wish. Leftover stuffing can be put in a custard cup to cook separately for the last 25 minutes.

4. Truss the birds and place on a rack in roasting pan. Roast 30 minutes. Meanwhile, heat the preserves with the ginger in a small saucepan; brush over the birds; roast 30 minutes longer, brushing with glaze until all is used and juices run clear when thigh is pierced.

FRUIT STUFFED CORNISH GAME HENS

Cooled and chilled, these are great to take on a picnic. When served hot, add Scalloped Potatoes (page 144), and Green Beans with Capers (page 132), and sherbet for dessert.

*1 medium-size apple, sliced, or 1 large navel orange, peeled
    and cut into segments*
1 small onion, roughly chopped
Salt and pepper
2 Cornish game hens (¾ pound each), thawed if frozen

APPLE GLAZE
¼ cup frozen apple juice concentrate
2 tablespoons honey
½ teaspoon dry mustard
2 tablespoons butter, softened

ORANGE GLAZE
¼ cup apricot preserves
2 tablespoons orange flavored liqueur or Rum Clement
2 tablespoons lemon juice

1. Preheat oven or toaster oven to 350 degrees.

2. Mix whichever fruit you choose with the onion. Season the insides of the birds with salt and pepper and stuff with the fruit mixture.

3. Truss the birds and place on a rack in a roasting pan. Roast for 30 minutes. Combine ingredients for either glaze in a small saucepan and bring to boiling. Brush over birds and roast for 30 minutes more, or until done, basting to use all the glaze. Birds are done when juices run clear when thigh is pierced.

SLIGHTLY GAMEY CHICKEN

For dinner in an hour, serve with Wild Rice (page 178), grapefruit and avocado salad, Stir-Fried Vegetables (page 151), Instant Crepe Dessert (page 210, if you have the crepes stashed in the freezer.

1 large, whole chicken breast (about 1¼ pounds), skinned, halved, and boned
Salt and pepper
1 tablespoon vegetable oil
1 tablespoon butter or margarine
1 tablespoon brandy, warmed
1 small onion, finely chopped
1 clove garlic, finely chopped
⅓ cup Madeira
½ cup heavy cream
1½ tablespoons drained, grated horseradish
¼ pound mushrooms, sliced
2 tablespoons butter

1. Preheat oven or toaster oven to 325 degrees.
2. Sprinkle chicken breasts with salt and pepper. Heat oil and 1 tablespoon butter in a medium-size skillet; sauté breasts until lightly browned on both sides.
3. Add brandy and ignite, shaking skillet until flames die out. Remove chicken to warm plate. Add onion and garlic to skillet and sauté 3 minutes or until tender but not browned. Return chicken to skillet.
4. Add Madeira; cover pan and simmer 8 minutes or until chicken is firm to the touch. If skillet is not ovenproof, transfer all to a baking dish. Combine cream and horseradish and pour over chicken. Cover and bake for 25 minutes.
5. Meanwhile, sauté the mushrooms in the remaining 2 tablespoons butter until browned. Scatter over chicken.

CHICKEN BREASTS WITH
WINE AND HERBS

For dinner in 30 minutes, serve with Confetti Rice (page 177), steamed broccoli, sliced tomato salad with basil dressing, and Frozen Chocolate Dessert (page 208).

1 large, whole chicken breast (about 1¼ pounds), skinned, halved, and boned
1 tablespoon vegetable oil
1 tablespoon butter or margarine
Salt and pepper
2 tablespoons lemon juice
½ cup dry white wine or vermouth
1 tablespoon chopped fresh tarragon or ½ teaspoon leaf, crumbled
1 tablespoon chopped fresh parsley

1. Remove any bits of fat from breasts. Heat the oil and butter in a medium-size heavy skillet. Brown chicken on all sides over medium heat. Sprinkle with salt and pepper.

2. Add lemon juice and wine, cover skillet, and cook for 8 minutes or until breasts feel firm to the touch. Remove to heated plates.

3. Add tarragon and parsley to skillet; bring to boil, stirring, and continue to cook while stirring, 3 to 4 minutes or until slightly thickened. Pour over chicken.

Note: This dish goes together so fast there is no point in doubling or tripling unless you prefer to shop infrequently.

CHICKEN WITH MUSTARD
AND CHEESE

For dinner in less than 30 minutes, serve with rice and steamed broccoli. This is the time to whip a Frozen Chocolate Dessert (page 208) out of the freezer.

3 tablespoons all-purpose flour
Salt and pepper
½ teaspoon paprika
1 large, whole chicken breast (about 1¼ pounds), halved
2 tablespoons vegetable oil
1 small onion, finely chopped
1 small clove garlic, finely chopped
1 stalk celery with leaves, diced
1 can (13¾ ounces) chicken broth
1 tablespoon country-style Dijon mustard
¼ cup freshly grated Gruyère or Swiss cheese
1 tablespoon chopped fresh parsley

1. On a piece of wax paper combine the flour, pinch of salt, pepper, and paprika. Coat the chicken breast halves with the flour mixture.

2. In a heavy casserole heat the oil and brown the breast halves on all sides; remove and reserve. Discard all but 1 tablespoon of the fat remaining in the casserole; add onion and garlic and sauté until tender but not browned. Add the celery and cook, stirring, 2 minutes.

3. Mix the broth gradually with the mustard and add mixture to casserole; return chicken breasts to casserole. Bring to a boil; cover and simmer 15 minutes or until chicken is done. Sprinkle each breast with half the cheese; sprinkle with parsley.

CHICKEN BREASTS WITH
ARTICHOKE HEARTS

This is a pale-colored, delicate dish that needs a mild-flavored but colorful vegetable such as yellow summer squash or boiled red-skinned new potatoes as an accompaniment. Add a salad and fresh fruit for dinner in less than 30 minutes.

3 tablespoons all-purpose flour
Salt and pepper
1 large, whole chicken breast (about 1 ¼ pounds), halved
2 tablespoons vegetable oil
1 medium-size onion, finely chopped
1 clove garlic, finely chopped
½ cup dry white wine
1 cup chicken broth
¼ teaspoon leaf thyme, crumbled
¼ teaspoon leaf rosemary, crumbled
1 can (14 ounces) artichoke hearts, drained, or 1 package (10 ounces) frozen
2 tablespoons chopped fresh parsley

1. On a piece of wax paper combine the flour, pinch of salt, and pepper. Coat the chicken breast halves with the flour mixture.

2. In a heavy casserole heat the oil and brown the breast halves on all sides; remove and reserve. Discard all but 1 tablespoon of the fat in the casserole and sauté the onion and garlic until tender but not browned.

3. Stir in wine and broth, thyme, and rosemary. Bring to a boil; return reserved chicken to casserole; add halved artichoke hearts. Bring to a boil; cover and simmer 15 minutes or until chicken is done. Sprinkle with parsley.

OVEN BARBECUED CHICKEN BREAST

Serve with corn on the cob, green salad, crusty bread, and Pears in Apricot Sauce (page 204), for dinner in just under an hour.

1 onion, finely chopped
1 clove garlic, crushed
¼ cup catsup
1 tablespoon cider vinegar
1 teaspoon Worcestershire sauce
⅓ cup water
2 teaspoons brown sugar
Salt and pepper
1 teaspoon chili powder
Dash liquid hot pepper seasoning
1 large, whole chicken breast (about 1¼ pounds), halved

1. In a small saucepan combine the onion, garlic, catsup, vinegar, Worcestershire, water, brown sugar, salt, pepper, chili powder, and hot pepper seasoning. Bring to a boil and simmer, uncovered, until barbecue sauce consistency, about 20 minutes.

2. Preheat oven or toaster oven to 375 degrees.

3. Brush the breast halves generously with the sauce and place in a shallow baking dish. Bake for 30 minutes, basting frequently with the sauce, or until chicken is tender and done.

CHICKEN WITH YOGURT

Serve with Wild Rice from the freezer in boil-in-the-bag (page 178), Zucchini Limone (page 150), and sliced oranges for dessert. Dinner can be ready in less than 30 minutes.

2 tablespoons vegetable oil
1 large, whole chicken breast (about 1¼ pounds), halved
1 medium-size onion, sliced into thin rings
1 teaspoon flour
2 teaspoons paprika
Salt and pepper
1 can (8 ounces) tomatoes
1 small sweet green pepper, cored, seeded and diced
1 container (8 ounces) plain yogurt
1 tablespoon chopped fresh parsley

1. Heat the oil in a heavy medium-size skillet. Brown the chicken on all sides; remove to paper towel.

2. Add onion rings to fat remaining in skillet and sauté until tender but not browned. Sprinkle with flour, paprika, salt, and pepper and cook 2 minutes, stirring constantly.

3. Add the tomatoes with their juice and return the chicken to the skillet; add green pepper; bring to a boil, cover and simmer 15 to 20 minutes or until chicken is tender. Move chicken to one side and stir in the yogurt and parsley. Reheat but do not boil.

GREEK CHICKEN BREAST

Serve with Lemon Rice (page 178), Puree of Peas (page 141), and Frozen Orange Mousse (page 202), from a cache in the freezer, and dinner can be ready in less than 30 minutes.

1 large, whole chicken breast (about 1¼ pounds), halved
1 tablespoon lemon juice
Salt and pepper
2 tablespoons vegetable oil
1 small onion, finely chopped
1 small clove garlic, finely chopped
½ small eggplant (about ¾ pound), peeled and cubed
2 plum tomatoes, skinned, seeded, and chopped
1 cup chicken broth
¼ cup dry white wine or vermouth
⅛ teaspoon ground cinnamon
⅛ teaspoon ground cloves
2 tablespoons chopped fresh parsley

1. Rub the chicken breast halves with the lemon juice; sprinkle lightly with salt and pepper. Heat the oil in a heavy casserole or saucepan and brown the chicken on all sides. Remove to paper towel.

2. Add the onion and garlic and eggplant and sauté until tender but not browned, about 4 minutes. Add more oil only if really necessary.

3. Add plum tomatoes, broth, wine, cinnamon, and cloves; bring to a boil; return chicken pieces, cover, and simmer 15 to 20 minutes or until chicken is tender. Sprinkle with parsley.

CHICKEN WITH MUSHROOMS

The texture of the mushrooms and the zip from the red pepper flakes make this chicken dish different. Serve it with noodles and green beans, tossed green salad, and Strawberry Mousse (page 206) for dessert. Dinner can be ready pronto!

3 tablespoons all-purpose flour
Salt and pepper
1 large, whole chicken breast (about 1¼ pounds), halved
2 tablespoons vegetable oil
1 medium-size onion, finely chopped
1 small clove garlic, finely chopped
¼ pound mushrooms, sliced
1 can (14½ ounces) no-salt-added stewed tomatoes
¼ teaspoon leaf thyme, crumbled
Pinch red pepper flakes
2 tablespoons chopped fresh parsley

1. On a piece of wax paper combine the flour, pinch of salt, and pepper. Coat the chicken breast halves with the flour mixture.

2. In a heavy casserole heat 1 tablespoon of the oil and brown the breast halves on all sides. Remove and reserve.

3. Sauté the onion and garlic in the fat remaining in the casserole until tender but not browned. Add the remaining tablespoon of oil and mushrooms and sauté 2 minutes.

4. Add tomatoes, thyme, and red pepper flakes; bring to boiling. Return chicken to casserole, cover, and simmer 15 minutes or until chicken is cooked. Sprinkle with parsley.

CHICKEN BREASTS CORDON BLEU
✕ ★ ■

For dinner in 30 minutes, serve with creamed spinach, carrot pennies, orange and red onion salad, frozen pound cake and raspberry sauce (puree a package of frozen raspberries and sieve to remove seeds).

> *1 large, whole chicken breast (about 1¼ pounds), skinned, halved, and boned*
> *1 thin slice well-flavored ham*
> *1 thin slice Swiss or Gruyère cheese*
> *1 teaspoon lemon juice*
> *Sauce Supreme (page 188)*
> *½ teaspoon Dijon mustard*
> *Paprika*

1. Preheat oven or toaster oven to 425 degrees.
2. Place breasts between sheets of wax paper and pound with a meat mallet, rolling pin, or heavy pan until thin; patch where meat tears.
3. Place half a slice of ham and half a slice of cheese on each breast. Roll up from the long side, tucking in the edges.
4. Place in a small buttered baking dish or individual dishes. Sprinkle with lemon juice. Cover tightly and bake for 15 minutes or until breasts feel firm to the touch. Remove to warm, heatproof plates.
5. Add mustard to Sauce Supreme and pour over chicken. Sprinkle with paprika and run under a preheated broiler to glaze, if you wish.

Note: Double or triple the recipe and wrap chicken tightly in foil and put sauce in small plastic containers or boil-in-the-bags and freeze for future quick dinners.

CHICKEN BREASTS DUXELLES
× ■

For dinner in under one hour, serve with hot cooked parsleyed rice, frenched green beans, Boston lettuce with Vinaigrette Dressing (page 171), with oatmeal cookies and ice cream for dessert.

1 large, whole chicken breast (about 1¼ pounds), skinned, halved, and boned
3 tablespoons Duxelles of Mushrooms (page 191)
1½ tablespoons butter or margarine
Salt
1 tablespoon lemon juice
2 mushroom caps
Sauce Supreme (page 188)

1. Preheat oven or toaster oven to 425 degrees.

2. Place chicken breast halves between sheets of wax paper. Pound with a meat mallet, rolling pin, or heavy pan until thin; patch where meat tears.

3. Spread flattened chicken with duxelles, leaving ¼ inch clear around the edges. Roll up starting with the long side, tucking in sides. Place side by side in a small baking dish or in 2 individual dishes. Dot with 1 tablespoon butter.

4. Sprinkle very lightly with salt and the lemon juice. Cover dish tightly and bake for 15 minutes or until firm and springy to the touch.

5. Remove to heated platter; pour over Sauce Supreme. Heat remaining ½ tablespoon butter in a small skillet and sauté the mushroom caps over high heat just until golden but still firm. Place a cap on each breast.

Note: Triple the recipe: eat one today and freeze the other two (omitting Sauce Supreme and mushroom caps) for quick dinners; or invite two guests on the spur of the moment.

CHICKEN BREASTS PARMESAN

For dinner in less than 30 minues, serve with spinach noodles, broiled, herbed tomato halves, hearts of lettuce with Russian dressing, and Pears in Apricot Sauce (page 204).

1 tablespoon vegetable oil
1 tablespoon butter or margarine
1 large, whole chicken breast (about 1¼ pounds), skinned, halved, and boned
½ teaspoon paprika
⅓ cup half-and-half or whole milk
2 egg yolks
½ teaspon Dijon-style mustard
¼ cup freshly grated Parmesan cheese
1 lemon slice, halved

1. Heat oil and butter in a medium-size skillet; sprinkle chicken with paprika and sauté in oil and butter until lightly browned on both sides.

2. Reduce heat and cook chicken until firm and springy to the touch, about 8 minutes. Place each chicken breast half in an individual au gratin dish or two in a larger one. Keep warm in a toaster oven set on low.

3. In a small saucepan combine the half-and-half, yolks, mustard, and 2 tablespoons of the Parmesan cheese. Cook while whisking over medium heat until thickened and smooth. Do not allow to boil.

4. Pour sauce over breasts; sprinkle with remaining Parmesan cheese. Broil until cheese melts and is golden. Garnish with lemon slices.

Note: If you buy boned chicken breasts, buy half a pound.

STIR-FRIED CHICKEN

Serve with Fried Rice (page 175), orange and avocado salad, and Flambéed Bananas (page 200) for dessert, for dinner in less than 30 minutes.

1 small, whole chicken breast (about ¾ pound), halved, skinned, boned, and cut into ½-inch pieces
3 tablespoons soy sauce
2 tablespoons dry sherry
2 teaspoons chopped fresh ginger root
2 teaspoons cornstarch
3 tablespoons vegetable oil
3 scallions, cut into ½-inch pieces
½ sweet green pepper, cored, seeded, and cut into ½-inch pieces
½ sweet red pepper, cored, seeded and cut into ½-inch pieces
1 cup bean sprouts
4 mushrooms, quartered
½ cup peas, thawed if frozen

1. Place chicken in a medium-size bowl; in a one-cup measure, combine 1 tablespoon of the soy sauce, the sherry, ginger, and cornstarch. Mix until smooth. Pour over the chicken and toss to coat.

2. Heat a wok or heavy skillet over high heat. Add 1 tablespoon of the oil; when oil shimmers, stir-fry the chicken until opaque, about 2 minutes. Push chicken to one side.

3. Add another tablespoon of oil. Add scallions and peppers and stir-fry 2 minutes. Add remaining tablespoon of oil, bean sprouts, mushrooms, and peas and stir-fry 1 minute, incorporating the chicken. Add remaining 2 tablespoons soy sauce and cook 1 minute.

CURRIED CHICKEN CREPES

★ |||||

This dish goes together fast if you have Basic Crepes (page 193) stored in the freezer. Serve with a green salad and crusty bread.

Sauce Supreme (page 188)
2 teaspoons curry powder, or to taste
1 cup diced cooked chicken or turkey
4 crepes, thawed (see Basic Crepe recipe, page 193)
2 tablespoons freshly grated Parmesan cheese

1. Preheat oven or toaster oven to 375 degrees.
2. Add the curry powder along with the flour in the Sauce Supreme recipe and cook, stirring, in the butter 1 to 2 minutes before proceeding.
3. Add enough of the curry sauce to the chicken to moisten well. Use curried chicken to fill the four crepes and place, seam side down, in 2 individual au gratin dishes or a shallow baking dish.
4. Make a band of the remaining curry sauce over the crepes; sprinkle with cheese and bake for 10 minutes or until bubbly hot. Run under a preheated broiler to glaze, if you wish.

CHICKEN POT PIES

× ■

If you are tired of chicken the same old way, make your own pot pies and enjoy with a mixed green salad and fresh fruit compote.

¾ cup chicken broth
1 boned chicken breast (8 to 12 ounces)
1 shallot, finely chopped
1½ tablespoons butter
1½ tablespoons flour
2 tablespoons heavy cream
Freshly ground black pepper
1 cup diced carrot and white turnip
½ cup frozen peas or 1 can (8¾ ounces) corn kernels, drained
½ stick pastry mix prepared according to label directions

1. Place the chicken broth and chicken breast in a small skillet; bring to a boil; cover and simmer 10 to 15 minutes or until the chicken is tender. Drain and reserve liquid. Skin chicken and cut into bite-size pieces.

2. Sauté the shallot in butter in a small saucepan until tender, about 3 minutes. Stir in the flour and cook, stirring, 1 minute. Gradually stir in the reserved chicken broth and cream. Bring to a boil, stirring constantly, and simmer 1 minute. Season to taste with pepper.

3. Cook carrot and white turnip in water barely to cover, in covered saucepan until barely tender, about 8 minutes. Drain.

4. Add the chicken pieces, carrot and turnip, and peas or corn to the sauce. Cool slightly.

5. Preheat oven or toaster oven to 425 degrees. Transfer chicken mixture to a 6$\frac{7}{16}$×4$\frac{3}{4}$×1$\frac{1}{2}$-inch oval foil pan or two individual tart pans (capacity 2$\frac{1}{2}$ cups).

6. Prepare the pastry and roll out on a lightly floured board to fit the top of the pie pan(s). Place over pans, turn under the edges and decorate. Make a steam hole. Bake for 30 minutes until the pastry is golden brown and filling bubbly hot.

Note: I often double this recipe, use my own start-from-scratch pastry, and freeze two unbaked pies for an emergency meal. Increase baking time of frozen pies to 40–45 minutes or until hot.

CHICKEN CURRY

⊙ ||||| ■

Any curry is an excuse to serve chutney, a real weakness of mine. Also add rice, cashews, currants, and chopped scallions. I serve mangoes or papayas for dessert. This is a great recipe for using up leftover turkey, too.

1 tablespoon butter
½ stalk celery, chopped
1 small tart apple, quartered, pared, cored, and diced
1 small onion, finely chopped
1 boneless chicken breast (12 to 16 ounces), cubed, or 1½
 cups cooked cubed chicken
2 teaspoons curry powder
2 teaspoons flour
¼ teaspoon ground ginger
¾ cup chicken broth
1 tablespoon chopped fresh parsley
Salt and pepper

1. Heat the butter in a small skillet and sauté the celery, apple, and onion until tender, about 3 minutes.

2. If using the raw chicken breast, turn up the heat, add the chicken, and stir-fry until chicken is tender, about 5 minutes.

3. Sprinkle with the curry powder, flour and ginger. Cook, stirring, 1 minute. Gradually stir in the chicken broth and bring to a boil, stirring. Add cooked chicken, if using, and simmer 5 to 10 minutes. Add parsley, salt, and pepper.

Note: This recipe freezes well in boil-in-the-bags, so double or quadruple, if you wish.

HOT CHICKEN MOUSSE

✕ ⊙ ⦀ ☼ ■

Serve with stir-fried snow peas, baked sweet potatoes, and Buttered Pears in Cream (page 204) for dessert.

2 cups cooked, boned, and skinned chicken, diced
½ cup light cream or half-and-half
1 egg white
¼ teaspoon ground nutmeg
Salt and pepper
1 tablespoon snipped fresh chives or 1 teaspoon freeze-dried
Blender Mushroom Sauce (page 188)

1. Preheat oven or toaster oven to 350 degrees.
2. Combine chicken, cream, and egg white in the container of an electric blender or food processor. Blend or whirl until smooth.
3. Add nutmeg, salt, pepper, and chives and blend or whirl to mix.
4. Turn into a well-buttered 8×4½×2½-inch loaf pan. Place loaf pan in a larger pan, place on oven rack, and pour hot water into the outer pan. Bake for 30 minutes or until firm.
5. Remove loaf pan from water and let stand 5 minutes. Unmold onto warm platter and serve with Blender Mushroom Sauce.

Note: As this loaf is good cold, I sometimes double the recipe and bake in a 9×5×3-inch loaf pan. Refrigerate to use within a couple of days or freeze for future use. Cooked turkey can also be used in place of chicken.

CHICKEN TACOS

IIIII

A pleasant alternate to ground beef tacos. Serve Avocado Halves with Spicy Sauce (page 7) as an appetizer, and Frozen Orange Mousse (page 202) for dessert, for a meal balanced in appearance, texture, and flavor.

1½ cups finely diced chicken, raw or cooked (1 large breast)
1 tablespoon vegetable oil
1 small onion, finely chopped
1 small clove garlic, finely chopped
1 tablespoon flour
1 tablespoon chili powder
1 teaspoon ground cumin
½ teaspoon leaf oregano, crumbled
½ cup hot enchilada sauce
Salt
1 tablespoon chopped fresh parsley
4 taco shells
¼ cup shredded Monterey Jack cheese
½ cup shredded lettuce

1. If the chicken is raw, place in a skillet with the oil, onion, and garlic and stir-fry until the chicken pieces are opaque and the onion tender. If the chicken is cooked, sauté the onion and garlic in the oil until tender and add the chicken.

2. Sprinkle flour, chili, cumin, and oregano over chicken mixture and cook, stirring, 3 minutes.

3. Add enchilada sauce and salt and cook, stirring occasionally, 10 minutes. Stir in parsley.

4. Preheat oven or toaster oven to 350 degrees and warm taco shells for 5 to 7 minutes. Fill each taco with ¼ of the chicken mixture, top with a tablespoon of the cheese and ¼ of the lettuce.

POLENTA WITH CHICKEN LIVERS

⊙

Serve with Marinated Vegetables (page 169) and Apple Crisp (page 198). Great for brunch.

1 cup water
¼ teaspoon salt
¼ cup yellow cornmeal
2 tablespoons vegetable oil
1 small onion, thinly sliced
1 medium-size green pepper, cored, seeded, and cut into strips
½ pound chicken livers, trimmed and cut in half
½ cup chicken broth
Salt and pepper
1 teaspoon cornstarch
¼ teaspoon leaf thyme, crumbled
1 tablespoon chopped fresh parsley

1. Heat ¾ cup water and the salt in a small (1-quart) saucepan until it boils. Meanwhile, mix the cornmeal with the remaining water until smooth; stir into the boiling water and continue to stir and cook, over low heat, until mush is very thick, about 5 minutes.

2. Divide the mush between 2 greased, individual, oval au gratin dishes (about 6 by 3⅓ inches on the bottom, holding 1½ to 2 cups). Set aside. Preheat oven or toaster oven to 350 degrees.

3. Heat 1 tablespoon of the oil in a small (8-inch) skillet and sauté the onion and green pepper 3 minutes. Remove with slotted spoon to a small bowl.

4. Add remaining oil to skillet and stir-fry the chicken livers over high heat until they are browned on the outside and still pink inside.

5. Combine the chicken broth, salt, pepper, cornstarch, and thyme in a 1-cup measure; stir to mix. Pour over the chicken livers and cook over medium heat while stirring, until sauce thickens and bubbles, about 1 minute.

6. Pour chicken liver mixture over the cornmeal mush, dividing

equally. Bake until hot, about 5 to 8 minutes. Sprinkle with the parsley.

Note: This dish is ideal for the chicken livers you have been saving in the freezer. Chicken livers are often sold in 1-pound packages; freeze the other ½ pound to prepare as above and serve with scrambled eggs for breakfast or brunch. Use in the next recipe or stir-fry them in butter, add salt, pepper, ¼ teaspoon leaf thyme, crumbled, 1 tablespoon Cognac, and 1 tablespoon chopped fresh parsley. Whirl mixture in a blender or food processor until smooth and serve with toast points or vegetable dippers for an appetizer.

CHICKEN LIVERS VICTORIA

Queen Victoria might have been surprised at what a dram of whiskey can do. Serve with hot cooked rice, Carrot Parsnip Puree (page 140) and fresh Fruit Compote (page 207) and Snapdragons (page 207), for dinner in less than 30 minutes.

½ pound chicken livers
1 tablespoon vegetable oil
1 tablespoon butter or margarine
Salt and pepper
2 tablespoons Scotch whiskey, warmed
1 shallot, finely chopped
1 small stalk celery, chopped
1 small tart apple, peeled, cored, and diced
¼ cup chicken broth
¼ cup light cream or half-and-half
2 tablespoons chopped fresh parsley

1. Trim bits of fat from livers and cut into halves. Heat the oil and butter in a medium-size heavy skillet. Add livers and sauté over medium-high heat, turning constantly, until browned on all sides, but still pink in the middle.

2. Sprinkle with salt and pepper, pour over whiskey, and ignite. Shake pan until flames have died down. Remove livers from skillet to a small bowl and reserve.

3. Add shallots, celery, and apple to skillet with an extra tablespoon of butter, if necessary, and sauté until soft. Return livers to skillet.

4. Add broth, reduce heat, cover, and simmer 10 minutes. Remove livers to warm plates. Add cream to skillet and reduce sauce by boiling over high heat until thickened. Pour sauce over livers and sprinkle with parsley.

Note: I save the livers from whole broiler-fryers in the freezer until I have 1/2 pound or I buy the market unit of one pound and freeze half for another time.

See Salads

for other great poultry dishes:

CHEF'S SALAD

CHICKEN AND GRAPE SALAD

BLACK-EYED PEAS SALAD

SMOKED TURKEY AND CHICK-PEA SALAD

ROAST HALF TURKEY BREAST
WITH VEGETABLES

Fresh turkey parts are a boon to two-member households. Serve with steamed broccoli, Boston lettuce and tomato salad, and fresh pears with cheese.

½ fresh turkey breast (1¾ to 2 pounds)
Salt and pepper
1 small onion, halved
Celery leaves
3 tablespoons margarine, melted, or vegetable oil
1 small butternut squash (¾ pound)
2 medium-size potatoes, peeled and very thinly sliced

1. Preheat oven or toaster oven to 350 degrees.
2. Season the turkey all over with salt and pepper. Place the onion and celery leaves under the rib cage and set the turkey breast in a small shallow roasting pan.
3. Pour the margarine or oil over the turkey. Peel squash, remove seeds and strings, and cut into 2-inch-size pieces. Add to roasting pan along with potato slices.
4. Roast for 1¼ to 1½ hours, basting with pan juices and turning the vegetables in the drippings.

Note: If you like cold turkey sandwiches or turkey leftover dishes, roast a whole turkey breast and add the vegetables halfway through the cooking.

BRAISED TURKEY DRUMSTICKS

⊙

This dish takes a little longer to cook than most but it is a hearty, flavorful, inexpensive main dish to serve with rice and Brussels sprouts and Strawberry Mousse (page 206).

2 tablespoons vegetable oil
2 turkey drumsticks (about 12 ounces each)
1 medium-size onion, finely chopped
1 clove garlic, finely chopped
1 carrot, diced
1 stalk celery with leaves, sliced
1 small white turnip, diced
1 can (13¾ ounces) chicken broth
Salt and pepper
½ teaspoon leaf thyme, crumbled
¼ teaspoon leaf marjoram, crumbled
2 tablespoons chopped fresh parsley

1. In a heavy oval casserole heat the oil and brown the drumsticks well on all sides; remove drumsticks and reserve.

2. Add the onion and garlic to the casserole and sauté until tender but not browned. Add the carrot, celery, and turnip and cook, stirring, 3 minutes.

3. Add the broth, salt, pepper, thyme, and marjoram; bring to a boil. Return drumsticks to casserole; cover and simmer 1 to 1¼ hours or until turkey is tender. Check the liquid level during cooking and add water if necessary.

Note: The same recipe can be used to cook turkey thighs and wings.

TURKEY ENCHILADAS

A mixed green salad and made-ahead Bread Pudding with Whiskey Sauce (page 211) make this dish into a meal.

2 tablespoons vegetable oil
½ pound ground raw turkey meat, thawed if frozen
2 scallions, finely chopped
½ cup plain yogurt
¼ teaspoon salt
½ can (4 ounces) chopped green chili peppers
4 corn tortillas
1 small onion, chopped
1 small clove garlic, chopped
¾ cup tomato puree
¼ teaspoon salt
½ cup grated Monterey Jack cheese

1. Heat 1 tablespoon of the oil in a small skillet and cook the turkey meat, stirring to break up, until all pink has disappeared.

2. Add the scallions, yogurt, salt, and chilies.

3. Warm the tortillas wrapped in foil in a toaster oven heated to 325 degrees for five minutes or wrapped in wax paper in the microwave for 30 seconds. Adding a drop or two of water before heating makes them more pliable.

4. Divide the turkey mixture between the tortillas and roll up. Place, seam side down, in two individual oval au gratin dishes. Preheat oven or toaster oven to 350 degrees.

5. Heat remaining oil in a small saucepan and sauté the onion and garlic until tender, about 2 minutes. Add the tomato puree and salt; bring to a boil and simmer 10 minutes. Pour over the enchiladas. Sprinkle with the Monterey Jack. Bake for 15 minutes or until hot and bubbly.

Note: The other half can of chilies can go into guacamole, a turkey meat loaf, or another Mexican favorite. Use extra tomato puree in Shrimp with Feta (page 41).

TURKEY CHILI
✕ ☀ ■

A tossed green salad with avocado and orange sections is all you need to round out this hearty main course.

1 small onion, finely chopped
1 small clove garlic, finely chopped
1 tablespoon vegetable oil
½ pound raw ground turkey meat, thawed if frozen
1 can (1 pound) plum tomatoes (2 cups)
1 tablespoon chili powder, or to taste
1 teaspoon flour
1 teaspoon ground cumin
¼ teaspoon ground ginger
Salt and pepper
½ can (20 ounces) kidney beans (1 cup, approximately)

1. Sauté the onion and garlic in the oil in a medium-size saucepan until tender, about 2 minutes.

2. Add the turkey and cook, stirring, until all signs of pink have disappeared and meat starts to brown slightly.

3. Add the tomatoes with their juice, chili powder, flour, cumin, ginger, salt, and pepper. Bring to a boil; cover and simmer 30 minutes.

4. Stir in the beans and reheat.

Note: This dish is best the second day or when it has had a chance to stand in the refrigerator at least 4 to 6 hours. This is another recipe that I double or quadruple because it keeps in the refrigerator several days or in the freezer in boil-in-the-bags for one to two months. I add the extra half can of beans to a spinach salad with bean sprouts, scallions and Vinaigrette Dressing (page 171).

TURKEY BREAKFAST SAUSAGE

◉

These patties can be served for breakfast or used in any recipe calling for sausages or sausage meat. Change the herb and you have a whole different product. Ground turkey is very bland, so it needs more seasonings than ground pork or beef.

½ pound ground raw turkey meat, thawed if frozen
½ teaspoon salt, or to taste
1 tablespoon chopped fresh sage or 1 teaspoon leaf, crumbled
¼ teaspoon pepper
¼ teaspoon hot pepper flakes
1 shallot, finely chopped
2 tablespoons butter

1. In a medium-size bowl combine the turkey, salt, sage, pepper, and pepper flakes. Mix well.

2. Sauté the shallot in the butter until tender, about 2 minutes. Add to the turkey mixture. The flavor is better if the mixture is refrigerated overnight before making into patties and pan-frying until cooked. Test a tiny piece of the sausage by pan-frying and tasting. Add more seasonings, if desired.

Note: Sometimes it is possible to buy 3-pound rolls of frozen raw ground turkey. Allow it to partially thaw, cut into 1/2 pound pieces with a frozen food saw or a good serrated knife. Wrap and freeze until needed. Use in Turkey Chili (page 81), Turkey Enchiladas (page 80), meat loaves, etc.

For a great way to use up

leftover turkey, see also

CHICKEN CURRY and HOT CHICKEN MOUSSE

ROAST DUCK WITH FRUIT STUFFING AND SAUCE

For a special occasion, serve with Wild Rice (page 178), steamed asparagus with butter sauce, and Strawberry Mousse (page 206).

1 duck (4½ to 5 pounds), thawed if frozen
Salt and pepper
3 tablespoons butter
1 small onion, finely chopped
1 stalk celery with leaves, diced
⅓ cup water
1 cup corn bread stuffing mix or crumbled corn bread
2 medium-size tart apples, peeled, cored, and diced
1 tablespoon chopped fresh sage or 1 teaspoon leaf, crumbled
2 tablespoons chopped fresh parsley
1 navel orange
1 lemon
2 tablespoons sugar
2 tablespoons distilled white vinegar
½ cup canned brown gravy
¾ cup chicken broth
2 tablespoons orange-flavored liqueur
2 tablespoons red currant or raspberry jelly

1. Preheat oven to 375 degrees.
2. Season the duck inside and out with salt and pepper.
3. Heat the butter in a small (8-inch) skillet and sauté the onion and celery 3 minutes. Add the water, stuffing mix, apples, sage, and parsley. Mix well. Season to taste with salt and pepper. Use to stuff the duck. With fine string tie legs and wings close to duck, prick all over with a two-tined fork, and set on a rack in a roasting pan.
4. Roast for 1½ to 2 hours or until the juices run clear when the thickest part of the thigh is pricked with a fork. Halfway through the roasting, pour off the accumulated fat.
5. Meanwhile, remove the orange- and lemon-colored peel from

the orange and half the lemon and cut into very thin slivers. Place in a small (1-quart) saucepan; cover with water. Bring to a boil; simmer 1 minute; drain and set aside.

6. In a small (6- to 8-inch) skillet, heat the sugar and vinegar, stirring until sugar dissolves. Boil gently until mixture turns a caramel color. Do not allow to burn.

7. Squeeze the orange and the lemon and combine the orange juice with 2 tablespoons of the lemon juice.

8. When the duck is cooked, pour off accumulated fat. Turn up the oven heat to 425 degrees to crisp the skin if you wish; watch carefully, it will only take about 10 minutes. Place the duck on a warm platter and keep warm.

9. Pour off remaining fat from the roasting pan; add the brown gravy and chicken broth and cook, stirring to scrape up all the browned-on bits. Add the caramel, citrus rinds, juice, liqueur, and jelly. Bring to a boil, stirring. Season with salt and pepper and serve separately.

Note: Half a duck is not too much for some people to eat; I usually serve the breast, stuffing, and sauce the first night; cut off the legs and reheat in the sauce another night, or freeze the legs and sauce separately to use within 2 months.

MEATS

BRAISED CHUCK STEAK

A green vegetable or mixed green salad is all this hearty dish needs. Sherbet with kiwi fruit makes a light, refreshing dessert. It is an under-30-minute dinner if a tender cut of chuck is used.

1 underblade, boneless chuck steak (about 12 ounces), all
 visible fat removed
1 tablespoon vegetable oil
1 small onion, finely chopped
1 clove garlic, finely chopped
2 carrots, scraped and cut into julienne strips.
1 can (14½ ounces) tomatoes with juice
½ teaspoon leaf thyme, crumbled
Salt and pepper
½ package (10 ounces) frozen tiny lima beans
1 tablespoon chopped fresh parsley

1. Brown the chuck steak quickly in the oil in a heavy casserole or Dutch oven. Remove and reserve.

2. Add the onion and garlic and sauté 3 to 4 minutes. Add the carrots and sauté 3 minutes longer. Return the meat to the casserole, add the tomatoes, thyme, salt, and pepper. Bring to a boil, add the lima beans, cover, and cook until meat and beans are tender, about 15 minutes. Sprinkle with parsley.

Note: This is a quick dinner when you don't want to embark on making a big pot of stew to freeze. Less tender cuts of chuck may take longer to cook.

SWISS PEPPERED STEAK

✕ ☀ ■

This dish reheats well so make it ahead and serve with Scalloped Potatoes (page 144) or Wild Rice (page 178), Baked Butternut Squash (page 148), and Baked Stuffed Apples (page 200) for dessert.

1 pound top or bottom round steak, ½ inch thick
1½ teaspoons peppercorns or coarsely cracked pepper
3 tablespoons vegetable oil
1 tablespoon brandy, warmed
1 onion, sliced
1 clove garlic, finely chopped
⅓ cup dry red wine
½ cup beef broth
2 tablespoons tomato paste
1 tablespoon butter
2 tablespoons chopped fresh parsley

1. Preheat oven or toaster oven to 350 degrees.

2. Trim the meat of all fat and divide in half. Crush the peppercorns in a mortar and pestle or by putting in a plastic bag and pounding with a meat pounder. Rub coarse pepper into meat on both sides.

3. Heat 2 tablespoons of the oil in a skillet and brown the meat on both sides. Pour brandy over, ignite, and shake pan until flames die out. Remove meat to a shallow baking dish.

4. Add remaining tablespoon oil to skillet and sauté onion and garlic until tender; scatter over meat. Add wine and broth to skillet; bring to a boil while scraping up browned-on bits. Pour over meat.

5. Cover and bake for 1½ hours or until tender. Remove meat to warm plates and pour liquid into a small saucepan; stir in tomato paste, bring to a boil, and cook until slightly reduced. Swirl in the butter gradually. Pour over meat and garnish with parsley.

Note: This recipe lends itself to doubling or quadrupling to freeze in boilable bags for a quick dinner.

SPICY STIR-FRIED BEEF

Serve with Fried Rice (page 175) or plain rice, Stir-Fried Vegetables (page 151), canned lychee and fortune cookies.

½ flank steak, cut lengthwise and weighing about 8 to 12
   ounces
2 tablespoons chili sauce
2 tablespoons light soy sauce
1 tablespoon dry sherry
1 teaspoon cornstarch
1 teaspoon finely chopped fresh ginger root
⅛ teaspoon hot pepper flakes
2 tablespoons vegetable oil
1 clove garlic, finely chopped
3 scallions, cut on the bias into 1-inch lengths

1. Freeze the half flank steak for 10 minutes. Cut the partially frozen steak across the grain in ⅛-inch pieces. They will be about 3 inches long.

2. Mix the chili sauce, soy sauce, sherry, cornstarch, ginger, and pepper flakes in a small bowl; set aside.

3. Heat 1 tablespoon of the oil in a wok or skillet; add garlic and scallions and stir-fry 1 minute. Remove to a small bowl with a slotted spoon.

4. Add remaining oil to wok and stir-fry the steak pieces over high heat until meat browns slightly and there is no sign of pink. Add to scallions in bowl.

5. Stir chili mixture until smooth and add to wok; heat, stirring, until bubbly hot. Stir in meat-scallion mixture and cook, stirring, until chili sauce mixture coats meat and everything is hot.

Note: The other half of the flank steak can be frozen for up to 3 months. Thawed and marinated, or pierced all over and sprinkled with nonseasoned tenderizer, it can be broiled for about 5 minutes a side. Cut at an angle across the grain to serve. Or, the flank steak can be used in Stir-Fried Orange Beef, the following recipe.

STIR-FRIED ORANGE BEEF

Serve with Fried Rice (page 175) or plain rice, sliced radish salad, and marinated orange slices for dinner in less than 30 minutes.

½ flank steak, cut lengthwise and weighing 8 to 12 ounces
2 tablespoons soy sauce
1 teaspoon cornstarch
1 tablespoon grated orange rind
1 tablespoon finely chopped fresh ginger root
4 tablespoons vegetable oil
1 sweet red pepper, cored, seeded, and cut into strips
4 scallions, cut on the bias into 1-inch pieces
2 ounces fresh snow peas or 1 cup broccoli flowerets
¼ cup sliced water chestnuts or bamboo shoots
⅛ teaspoon red pepper flakes

1. Freeze the half flank steak for 10 minutes. Cut the partially frozen steak across the grain into ⅛-inch pieces. They will be about 3 inches long.

2. In a custard cup combine the soy sauce, cornstarch, orange rind, and ginger; set aside.

3. Heat 2 tablespoons oil in a wok or skillet. Add the meat pieces and stir-fry over high heat for 5 minutes or until slightly browned and no pink is visible. Remove with slotted spoon to a paper towel–lined dish.

4. Add the remaining 2 tablespoons of oil to the wok and stir-fry the red peppers and scallions 3 minutes; add snow peas or broccoli and stir-fry 2 minutes longer. Add water chestnuts and red pepper flakes.

5. Stir the cornstarch mixture until smooth and add to the wok while stirring. Cook over medium heat until mixture thickens and bubbles. Stir in the reserved meat. Heat until vegetables and meat are coated and hot.

Note: I broil the other half of the flank steak after marinating it, or piercing all over with a fork and sprinkling with nonseasoned tenderizer. Broiling takes only about 5 minutes a side. Slice at an angle across the grain. Or, use it in Spicy Stir-Fried Beef, the preceding recipe. Properly wrapped, it will keep in the freezer for three months.

SYMBOLS

As you flip through this cookbook you will see one or more symbols beside most of the recipes. These are provided for your ease in finding a dish best suited to the needs of any particular day or week. If you have some extra time on a weekend, for example, there are recipes that can be made ahead and frozen. If you have to have a meal on the table quickly, there are over fifty combinations indicated that can be prepared in less than thirty minutes. Here are brief descriptions of what the eight different symbols mean:

✕   This recipe can be *doubled* easily.

⊙   *Versatile.* This recipe can be adapted to different parts of the menu (e.g., appetizer, main dish, or side dish), or to different ingredients (e.g., chicken or turkey).

★   *Quick.* This recipe and the suggested accompaniments (with some freezer backups) can be on the table in under thirty minutes.

‖‖‖   This recipe is good for using up *leftovers.*

✍   *Seasonal.* This recipe is especially appropriate or possible only during a particular season.

☼   This recipe can be, or is best when, *made ahead.*

■   This recipe can be *frozen.* Reheat in a conventional oven or a microwave oven, where applicable.

🐝   *Elegant.*

STUFFED MEAT LOAF

Serve with oven-browned potatoes, green beans with mushrooms, and sherbet. This recipe makes two loaves for two meals; see note.

1 pound ground lean beef
¾ cup soft bread crumbs
½ cup milk
2 shallots, finely chopped
¼ cup chopped fresh parsley
1 tablespoon chopped fresh basil, or 1 teaspoon leaf basil, crumbled
2 teaspoons chopped fresh oregano or ½ teaspoon leaf oregano, crumbled
1 egg, lightly beaten
Pepper
Unseasoned dry bread crumbs
4 ounces thinly sliced ham
4 ounces thinly sliced Swiss or Gruyère cheese

1. Combine the beef, soft bread crumbs, milk, shallots, parsley, basil, oregano, egg, and pepper in a medium-size bowl. Mix well.

2. Preheat oven or toaster oven to 350 degrees.

3. Divide the meat mixture in half. Pat out each half on a piece of wax paper, lightly sprinkled with dry bread crumbs, into an 8×7-inch rectangle.

4. Arrange half the ham and then half the cheese slices over each rectangle, leaving a ½-inch border clear all around. Using the wax paper as an aid, roll the rectangles, starting with the short side, like a jelly roll. Pinch ends to close. Place on a jelly roll pan (15×10×1 inches) and bake for 1 hour.

Note: I serve one roll hot immediately; the second one can be refrigerated and served cold with salad another night or used as a sandwich filling. Or, it can be frozen to eat hot or cold within two months.

STUFFED CABBAGE
✕ ■

I find this a filling main course that only needs a boiled potato and Apple Crisp (page 198) for dessert.

½ small cabbage (8 to 12 ounces)
1 small onion, finely chopped
1 clove garlic, finely chopped
2 tablespoons vegetable oil
½ pound lean ground beef
½ cup cooked rice (¼ cup raw cooked according to label directions)
Salt and pepper
1 tablespoon snipped fresh dillweed or ½ teaspoon dried
1 can (15 ounces) tomato sauce

1. Place the cabbage in a saucepan of boiling water and simmer 5 minutes or until leaves separate easily. Drain.

2. Meanwhile, sauté the onion and garlic in the oil in a small skillet. Add the ground beef and cook, stirring, until all pink has disappeared. Preheat oven or toaster oven to 350 degrees.

3. Add the rice, salt, pepper, and dill to skillet and mix well.

4. Separate the cabbage leaves into 4 to 6 bundles. Divide the meat mixture between the bundles and roll up each to enclose the meat mixture. Set, seam side down, in a baking dish. Pour over the tomato sauce, cover, and bake for 35 minutes.

Note: If you are in the mood, double the recipe, refrigerate tightly covered, and then freeze half for a second meal. If not, plan to serve Cole Slaw with Peppers and Pickles (page 162) or Braised Cabbage with Caraway Seeds (page 134) to use the rest of the cabbage.

MEAT BALLS

■

Serve with Well-Seasoned Tomato Sauce (page 187) and spaghetti, green salad, and Flambéed Bananas (page 200). This recipe makes enough meat balls for two meals.

2 tablespoons butter or margarine
1 small onion, finely chopped
½ cup soft bread crumbs
½ cup water or milk
1 pound extra lean ground beef
Salt and pepper
⅛ teaspoon nutmeg
1 teaspoon chopped fresh oregano or ¼ teaspoon leaf, crumbled
2 tablespoons vegetable oil

1. In a small skillet heat the butter and sauté the onion until tender, about 2 minutes.

2. In a medium-size bowl soak the bread crumbs in the water.

3. Add the meat, cooked onion, salt, pepper, nutmeg, and oregano. Mix well. Form into 12 to 14 meat balls.

4. Heat the oil in a skillet and cook the meat balls until well browned all over and cooked through, about 10 minutes. Drain on paper towel. Use half for dinner; refrigerate and then freeze the remaining meat balls for a quick dinner another night.

PORK WITH PEARS

This is a slow-cooking dish for a lazy winter weekend, so count on 1½ hours from start to finish if you serve it with Rice and Peas Venetian Style (page 142), mixed green salad with Vinaigrette Dressing (page 171), and Apple Almond Tarts (page 197), which can be made first and removed from the oven when done, allowing pork chops to continue cooking.

2 thick loin pork chops, well trimmed
Salt and pepper
½ teaspoon ground ginger
1 tablespoon vegetable oil
2 firm winter pears
1 tablespoon lemon juice
½ teaspoon cinnamon
3 tablespoons brown sugar
4 teaspoons butter or margarine
¼ cup dry vermouth

1. Preheat oven or toaster oven to 350 degrees.

2. Rub chops with salt, pepper, and ginger on both sides. Heat oil in skillet and brown chops on both sides. Remove chops to a baking dish large enough to accommodate chops and pear halves in a single layer.

3. Cut pears in half; peel and remove cores. Place pears, cut side up, in baking dish and sprinkle with lemon juice. Mix cinnamon and sugar and sprinkle over chops and pears. Place a teaspoon of butter in each pear cavity.

4. Pour vermouth around chops. Cover and bake for 40 minutes; remove cover and cook 10 minutes longer or until chops are tender and cooked through.

PORK CUTLETS NORMANDY

For dinner in less than an hour, serve with boiled new potatoes,
Brussels sprouts, Cole Slaw with Peppers and Pickles (page 162),
and Flambéed Bananas (page 200) for dessert.

1 tablespoon vegetable oil
1 tablespoon butter or margarine
2 boneless pork cutlets (6 to 8 ounces each), well trimmed
Salt and pepper
3 tablespoons apple brandy (Calvados or apple jack)
¼ cup apple cider or apple juice
1 apple, peeled, cored, and cut into 8 wedges
¼ cup half-and-half or heavy cream

1. Heat oil and butter in a deep heavy skillet. Season pork cutlets
with salt and pepper and brown on both sides in oil and butter
mixture.

2. Warm brandy in a metal cup; pour over cutlets, ignite, and
shake pan until flame dies. Add cider and apple wedges to skillet.

3. Cover skillet and simmer 35 to 40 minutes or until cutlets are
cooked through. Remove cutlets and apple to warm plates.

4. Add cream to skillet and reduce by boiling over high heat
until sauce thickens. Pour over cutlets and apples.

SMOKED PORK CHOPS WITH RED CABBAGE AND APPLES

This is one of the fastest meals I make, but it remains a favorite served with a spinach, mushroom and onion salad. Pears and cheese make a compatible dessert.

1 medium-size potato, sliced paper thin (easy with a food processor)
1 jar (16 ounces) sweet-sour red cabbage
2 smoked pork chops (6 ounces each)
1 tart apple, quartered, peeled, cored, and diced

1. Place the potato and cabbage in a medium-size skillet. Cover, bring to a boil, and simmer 10 minutes.

2. Add the pork chops and apple; cover and simmer 15 minutes longer or until chops are hot through and the potato is tender.

Note: A 6-ounce pork chop is ample for most pepole but if you are catering to a hearty appetite, throw in an extra chop.

SHREDDED PORK WITH SCALLIONS
AND SPROUTS

Serve this with Fried Rice (page 175) or plain rice and fresh pineapple for dessert for dinner in less than 30 minutes.

3 tablespoons vegetable oil, approximately
½ pound boneless pork cut into ⅛×2-inch slices with the grain
Vegetable oil
1 small sweet red pepper, cored, seeded, and cut into strips
4 scallions cut into 2-inch pieces
1 clove garlic, finely chopped
1 tablespoon chopped fresh ginger root
1½ cups tiny broccoli flowerets
½ cup chicken broth
1 tablespoon dry sherry
1 tablespoon cornstarch
¼ pound fresh bean sprouts or a 14-ounce can, drained and rinsed

1. Heat 1 tablespoon oil in a wok or skillet. Stir-fry the pork pieces until no pink remains, adding more oil if necessary. With a slotted spoon, transfer the pork to a bowl and keep warm.

2. Add another tablespoon of oil to the wok and stir-fry the red pepper, scallion, garlic, and ginger 2 to 3 minutes. Transfer to the bowl with a slotted spoon.

3. Add another tablespoon of oil to the wok, if necessary, and stir-fry the broccoli for 2 minutes. Add ¼ cup of the chicken broth. Cover and cook briefly for 3 minutes.

4. Meanwhile, mix the remaining chicken broth, sherry, and cornstarch together until smooth. Return the pork and vegetables to the wok. Stir in the cornstarch mixture and cook, stirring, until sauce thickens and coats the pieces. Stir in the bean sprouts. Reheat while stirring.

SPARE RIBS FOR TWO

■

Corn, Scalloped Potatoes (page 144), and a mixed green salad complement the ribs. If it's summertime, a ripe juicy peach or nectarine would make a fine dessert.

1½ to 2 pounds spare ribs
2 tablespoons finely chopped onion
2 teaspoons vegetable oil
1 tablespoon cider vinegar
1 tablespoon light brown sugar
2 tablespoons lemon juice
½ cup catsup
1 tablespoon Worcestershire sauce
1 teaspoon Dijon mustard
¼ cup water

1. Preheat oven or toaster oven to 450 degrees.
2. Place ribs on broiler rack and bake 30 minutes.
3. Meanwhile, sauté the onion in the oil in a small saucepan. Add vinegar, brown sugar, lemon juice, catsup, Worcestershire, mustard, and water. Bring to a boil and simmer 15 minutes. Reduce oven heat to 300 degrees.
4. Drain fat from broiler pan and return ribs to pan without rack. Brush both sides with barbecue sauce. Bake 30 minutes, turning and basting with sauce every 10 minutes.
5. Cut ribs into sections; brush with sauce and bake 15 minutes longer.

Note: Ask for a small order of ribs if there are none in the meat case. If you enjoy barbecued foods, double or quadruple the sauce recipe and store in the refrigerator for one week or in the freezer for three months.

SAUSAGE AND PEPPERS WITH SPAGHETTI

✕ ★ ■

For a 30-minute dinner, serve with a mixed green salad, hot garlic bread, and broiled grapefruit halves.

¾ to 1 pound veal sausage or Italian sausage, mixed sweet and hot
1 small onion, finely chopped
2 cloves garlic, finely chopped
2 medium-size sweet green peppers, or 4 Italian peppers, cored, seeded, and cut into ½ inch strips
1 can (15 ounces) thick tomato sauce
½ teaspoon leaf basil, crumbled
½ teaspoon leaf oregano, crumbled
Salt and pepper
½ pound spaghetti, cooked al dente, *drained*
Grated Parmesan cheese

1. Remove casings from sausages and cut into 1-inch lengths. Sauté in a medium-size skillet until browned on all sides.

2. Remove all but 2 tablespoons of the fat. Sauté onion and garlic in the 2 tablespoons of fat for 3 minutes. Add pepper strips and cook, stirring, 3 minutes.

3. Add tomato sauce, basil, oregano, salt and pepper. Bring to a boil; cover and simmer 10 minutes. Serve over spaghetti and pass the cheese separately.

Note: I usually double this recipe of sausage and peppers because it freezes well in boilable bags and offers a quick meal from the freezer on a busy day.

SAUSAGE AND POTATO SKILLET

Dinner can be ready in 30 minutes if you serve a green salad and fresh fruit for dessert.

1 tablespoon vegetable oil
1 medium-size onion, sliced and rings separated
4 medium-size potatoes (1¼ pounds), boiled, peeled, and sliced
Salt and pepper
¼ cup vinegar
8 ounces brown-and-serve pork sausages or fully cooked kielbasa (smoked sausage), sliced
6 ounces plain yogurt
2 tablespoons chopped fresh parsley

1. Heat the oil in a medium-size skillet and sauté the onion until tender; add potatoes, salt, pepper, and vinegar; bring to a boil.
2. Cut sausages into thirds and add to skillet; cook to heat sausages. Stir in yogurt and reheat but do not boil. Stir in parsley.

QUICK BAKED BEANS WITH SMOKED GARLIC SAUSAGE

This is a hearty main dish to serve with a green salad and garlic bread.

1 can (1 pound) small baked beans
1 small onion, finely chopped
1 tablespoon brown sugar
¼ teaspoon dry mustard
½ to ¾ pound smoked garlic sausage or cooked kielbasa

1. Preheat toaster or regular oven to 350 degrees.
2. In a 1½-quart casserole or baking dish combine the baked beans, onion, brown sugar, and dry mustard. Slice the sausage thinly and arrange on top of beans. Cover tightly with aluminum foil and bake 20 minutes. Uncover and bake 15 minutes longer.

CIDER GLAZED HAM STEAK
WITH YAMS

Have dinner in 30 minutes by serving this and Romaine with Creamy Blue Cheese Dressing (page 170), and peeled, sliced oranges marinated in orange flavored liqueur for dessert.

12 to 16 ounces fully cooked, smoked ham steak
⅓ cup apple cider or apple juice
2 tablespoons honey
2 tablespoons dark rum
1 can (9 ounces) yams or sweet potatoes in syrup
1 tart apple, quartered, cored, and peeled

1. Preheat oven or toaster oven to 375 degrees.
2. Place the ham in a shallow baking dish.
3. In a small saucepan combine cider, honey, and rum and heat, stirring until well blended; pour mixture over ham. Arrange drained yams and apple pieces around ham. Bake 25 minutes, basting several times.

Another ham main dish is

HAM AND LIMA BEAN SALAD

in Salads

HAM AND CHEESE ROLLS

Pick up the ingredients for this meal at the deli and have dinner on the table in less than 30 minutes when you serve the rolls with linguine, steamed broccoli, and Peach Syllabub (page 203).

4 slices ham, ¼ inch thick
4 slices Swiss or Gruyère cheese
½ cup ricotta cheese
Pepper
½ teaspoon leaf oregano, crumbled
1 tablespoon chopped fresh parsley
2 teaspoons snipped fresh chives or ½ teaspoon freeze-dried
1 cup Well-Seasoned Tomato Sauce (page 187)
2 tablespoons freshly grated Parmesan cheese
2 tablespoons unflavored dry bread crumbs

1. Preheat oven or toaster oven to 400 degrees. Line up the ham slices on a board; top each with a slice of cheese.

2. In a small bowl mix together the ricotta, pepper, oregano, parsley, and chives. Divide ricotta mixture among the ham/cheese stacks; spread to within ½ inch of edges; roll up and place seam side down in a single layer in a buttered baking dish.

3. Pour tomato sauce over rolls; mix Parmesan and crumbs and sprinkle over sauce. Bake 15 minutes or until sauce is bubbly.

ROAST LEG OF LAMB

Those of us who cook for two on a regular basis often crave a roast; I like to buy a half leg of lamb and enjoy it with flageolets or white beans and Broccoli Puree (page 133). I divide the leftovers to have 2 to 3 cups of tiny cubes for Curried Lamb (page 106), and I grind the remainder for Lamb with Feta Cheese and Spinach (page 105).

1 half leg lamb (about 4 to 5 pounds) (I prefer the shank end)
1 large clove garlic, cut into slivers
Salt and pepper
1 teaspoon leaf rosemary, crumbled

1. Preheat oven to 325 degrees.

2. With a sharp knife remove the fell (thin skin) from over the fat and trim some of the excess fat away. With the point of a knife make slits all over the surface and insert a sliver of garlic in each slit.

3. Season roast with salt and pepper and rub all over with rosemary. Place on a rack in a roasting pan and roast for about 20 minutes a pound for medium-rare. Test with a meat thermometer in the meatiest portion away from bone and fat; it should register 125 to 130 degrees for rare; temperature will rise another 10 to 15 degrees on standing 15 minutes before carving.

GROUND LAMB WITH FETA CHEESE AND SPINACH
★ ⊙ IIIII

Whether you start with leftover cooked leg of lamb or fresh ground lamb, it is a tasty dish for lunch or dinner. Start with Chilled Cucumber Soup (page 19) and have fresh fruit for dessert. The meal is ready in less than 30 minutes.

½ pound ground lamb or 2 cups leftover, cooked, ground
*   Roast Leg of Lamb (page 104), plus 1 tablespoon butter*
1 small onion, finely chopped
1 small clove garlic, finely chopped
1 small sweet green pepper, seeded, cored, and diced
1 tablespoon finely chopped fresh parsley
½ teaspoon leaf oregano, crumbled, or 1 tablespoon chopped
*   fresh mint*
½ cup crumbled feta cheese
½ bag (10 ounces) washed fresh spinach or ½ pound fresh
Salt and pepper
2 whole-wheat pita bread

1. In a medium-size heavy skillet brown the ground lamb, stirring to break up the lumps, until no sign of pink remains, or heat the cooked lamb in the butter.

2. Add the onion, garlic and green pepper to the skillet and cook, stirring often, until vegetables are tender but not browned.

3. Add the parsley, oregano and feta. Trim and wash the spinach and cook in the water clinging to the leaves until wilted. Drain well and squeeze out excess moisture. Add to skillet with salt and pepper; reheat mixture. Warm pita bread briefly; halve and fill with lamb mixture.

CURRIED LAMB

IIIII ☼

I make this with half the leftovers from roasting the half Roast Leg of Lamb (page 104). I serve it with rice, chutney, and a green salad with exotic fruit like papayas or mangoes for dessert.

1 medium-size apple, peeled, cored, and diced.
1 stalk celery, diced
1 medium-size onion, finely chopped
2 tablespoons vegetable oil
1½ tablespoons curry powder, or to taste
1 teaspoon ground ginger
1 tablespoon flour
1 can (13¾ ounces) chicken broth
2 to 3 cups cooked cubed lamb
¼ cup raisins
¼ cup slivered blanched almonds

1. In a medium-size skillet sauté the apple, celery, and onion in the oil until tender. Sprinkle with the curry powder, ginger, and flour. Cook, stirring, 2 to 3 minutes.

2. Stir in the broth; bring to a boil; add lamb and raisins. Simmer 10 minutes. Set aside to allow flavors to meld for at least 30 minutes or in the refrigerator several hours, or overnight, before reheating. Sprinkle with almonds before serving.

LAMB HOTPOT

Here's a dinner in a pot that can be made ahead when you have 30 minutes to put it together and something else to do while it cooks for 1½ hours. Refrigerate until serving time. Dinner can be ready in 15 minutes if you make Spinach, Mushroom and Feta Salad (page 167), and bake an Apple Crisp (page 198) at the same time you reheat the Hotpot.

1 tablespoon vegetable oil
2 shoulder lamb chops (1 inch thick), well trimmed
1 medium-size onion, sliced into rings
1 clove garlic, finely chopped
1 potato, peeled and thinly sliced
Salt and pepper
½ teaspoon leaf thyme, crumbled
½ navel orange
1 cup dry red wine or chicken broth
2 large carrots, cut into julienne strips
½ package (10 ounces) frozen peas or 1 cup loose

1. Preheat oven or toaster oven to 350 degrees. Heat the oil in a medium-size skillet and brown the chops on both sides; remove and reserve. Sauté the onion and garlic in the skillet until tender but not browned.

2. Place potatoes in the bottom of a greased shallow baking dish; cover with onions. Place chops on top of onions and sprinkle with salt, pepper, and thyme.

3. Remove seeds from orange; cut in half again and place in container of electric blender or food processor; whirl or process until finely chopped. Pour over chops.

4. Pour in wine and scatter carrots over all. Cover tightly and bake for 1½ hours. If you plan to serve immediately, add the peas 10 minutes before serving or, if you are making ahead, add the peas as you reheat the dish in a 400-degree oven for 15 minutes or until bubbly.

BRAISED LAMB SHANKS

Serve with Wilted Spinach (page 147) and noodles or rice, with sliced oranges marinated in orange-flavored liqueur for dessert.

2 tablespoons flour
Salt and pepper
2 small (½ to ¾ pound each) lamb shanks
2 tablespoons olive oil
1 clove garlic, finely chopped
1 small onion, finely chopped
½ teaspoon leaf thyme, crumbled
1 can (14½ ounces) stewed tomatoes
1 cup chicken broth
½ pound eggplant, peeled and cut into 1-inch cubes

1. Combine the flour, salt, and pepper in a plastic bag. Add the shanks and toss to coat.

2. Heat the oil in a heavy casserole or Dutch oven. Brown the shanks on all sides; remove and reserve.

3. Add the garlic and onion to the casserole and sauté 3 minutes, stirring often. Return the shanks to the casserole. Add thyme, tomatoes, chicken broth, and eggplant to the casserole. Bring to a boil; cover and simmer 1 hour or until shanks are tender.

LAMB BREAST WITH LENTILS

I make this ahead so that it has time to chill in the refrigerator and it is easy to lift off the fat. Tastes delicious but it needs some bright greens such as creamed spinach or Boston lettuce and tomato salad to perk up the appearance. Grapes are a good choice for dessert.

1½ pounds lamb flank or breast, bone-in and well trimmed
* of fat*
1 small onion, finely chopped
1 clove garlic, finely chopped
1 stalk celery, diced
1 carrot, diced
½ cup lentils, picked over and washed
1 can (13¾ ounces) chicken broth
½ teaspoon leaf rosemary, crumbled
Salt and pepper
¾ cup frozen peas
1 tablespoon chopped fresh parsley

1. In a heavy casserole or Dutch oven brown the meat on all sides. Remove and reserve. Pour out all but 1 tablespoon of fat.

2. Add the onion and garlic and sauté until tender. Add the celery and carrot and sauté 3 minutes longer.

3. Add the reserved meat, lentils, broth, rosemary, salt and pepper. Bring to a boil; cover and simmer 50 minutes or until lentils and meat are tender.

4. Add the peas; cover and cook 5 minutes. Sprinkle with parsley.

Note: I find so many uses for celery, carrots and onions in the course of a week, I don't have to plan on using them up. I keep a polybag of frozen peas to dip into and I use lentils in soup (see page 21) and salads, so a 1-pound bag goes fast. Cooked lentils with smoked sausage is a great dish too.

LAMB CHOPS TERIYAKI WITH RICE

For dinner in 30 minutes, not counting marinating time, serve with stir-fried broccoli with mushrooms and Peach Syllabub (page 203) for dessert.

2 shoulder lamb chops (¾ to 1 inch thick), well trimmed
1 clove garlic, finely chopped
1 tablespoon honey
¼ teaspoon dry mustard
½ teaspoon ground ginger
Pepper
2 tablespoons lemon juice or dry sherry
¼ cup vegetable oil
¼ cup soy sauce
½ cup long grain rice, cooked according to label directions

1. Place chops in a deep glass or ceramic dish in a single layer. In a small bowl combine garlic, honey, mustard, ginger, pepper, lemon juice, oil, and soy sauce; pour over chops and marinate in the refrigerator 8 hours or overnight, turning occasionally if practical.

2. Remove chops from marinade and place on broiler rack; pour marinade into a small saucepan and heat.

3. Broil about 4 inches from heat for 7 minutes on each side. Stir hot marinade into hot cooked rice and serve with chops.

VEAL PICCATA

For dinner in 30 minutes, serve with Lemon Rice (page 178), Puree of Peas (page 141), marinated artichoke hearts on lettuce, and raspberry sherbet for dessert.

1 tablespoon vegetable oil
2 tablespoons butter or margarine
8 ounces veal scallops*
Salt and pepper
2 tablespoons lemon juice
¼ cup dry white wine or vermouth
1 tablespoon chopped fresh parsley

1. Heat the oil and 1 tablespoon of the butter in a medium-size skillet. Brown the scallops quickly on both sides over medium-high heat. Season with salt and pepper. Add 1 tablespoon of the lemon juice and the wine. Reduce heat; cover pan and simmer 3 minutes.

2. Remove veal to heated plates. Bring liquid in skillet to a boil; add remaining butter and lemon juice and cook, stirring, until liquid is syrupy; pour over veal; sprinkle with parsley.

* Or substitute pounded, boned chicken or turkey breast slices.

VEAL STEW WITH PEPPERS AND RICE
✕ ☀ ■

For a make-ahead dinner, fix the stew the day before along with Eggplant Parmigiana (page 137), Marinated Vegetables (page 169), and Bread Pudding with Whiskey Sauce (page 211).

1 tablespoon vegetable oil
1 tablespoon butter or margarine
¾ pound stewing veal, trimmed and cut into 1-inch pieces
1 small onion, sliced
½ sweet green pepper, cored, seeded, and diced
½ sweet red pepper, cored, seeded, and diced
2 teaspoons paprika
¼ cup vermouth
1 cup chicken broth
Salt and pepper
2 sprigs parsley
1 teaspoon leaf thyme, crumbled
1 bay leaf
½ cup long-grain rice
2 tablespoons butter or margarine, melted
¼ cup fine unflavored dry bread crumbs
2 tablespoons pine nuts

1. Preheat oven or toaster oven to 325 degrees.

2. Heat oil and butter in a heavy skillet and brown the veal on all sides. Remove with slotted spoon to a bowl.

3. Sauté onion and green and red pepper until tender, adding more oil if needed. Sprinkle paprika over vegetables and stir in.

4. Add vermouth, broth, salt, pepper, parsley, thyme, and bay leaf. Bring to a boil. Add veal.

5. Turn into a heavy casserole. Cover and bake 1¼ hours or until meat is tender. Stir in rice, cover, and cook 25 minutes longer or until rice is tender and liquid has been absorbed.

6. Combine melted butter, bread crumbs and pine nuts; sprinkle over meat and rice and run under the broiler to brown.

Note: This is a great recipe to double or quadruple and freeze in boil-in-the-bags for quick-fix meals anytime.

VEAL STEW WITH MUSHROOMS

✕ ■

Thin egg noodles and frenched green beans are nice with this stew. Add a simple Boston lettuce salad with a good homemade Vinaigrette Dressing (page 171) and individual fruit tarts.

1 pound veal shoulder, cut into 1-inch cubes
3 tablespoons olive oil
1 large onion, finely chopped
1 clove garlic, finely chopped
4 ounces mushrooms, sliced
2 small sweet red peppers, cored, seeded, and cut into chunks
Salt and pepper
⅓ cup vermouth
1 cup chicken broth
½ teaspoon leaf rosemary, crumbled
2 teaspoons cornstarch
¼ cup water

1. Brown the veal in the oil in a heavy casserole or Dutch oven. Remove with a slotted spoon to a bowl and keep warm.

2. Sauté the onion and garlic in the oil remaining in the casserole until tender, about 4 minutes. Add the mushrooms and red pepper and cook, stirring, until mushrooms brown slightly.

3. Return the veal to the casserole; season with salt and pepper. Add the vermouth, chicken broth, and rosemary; bring to a boil; cover and simmer about 1½ hours or until meat is tender.

4. Mix the cornstarch with the water. Add a little of the hot broth from the stew to the cornstarch mixture. Mix well and return all to the casserole. Cook, stirring, until mixture thickens and bubbles.

Note: This is good to make on a weekend for Monday or Tuesday night's dinner. Double or quadruple the recipe and freeze in individual portions in boil-in-the-bags and they are ready to eat in 15 minutes for one or two. No pot to wash, either.

OSSO BUCO

Serve with noodles, green beans, marinated artichoke salad, and rum trifle.

1 tablespoon flour
Salt and pepper
1 veal shank (about 1 pound)
2 tablespoons oil
1 clove garlic, finely chopped
1 small onion, finely chopped
1 carrot, diced
½ cup dry white wine or vermouth
½ cup Well-Seasoned Tomato Sauce (page 187)
1 cup water
1 tablespoon chopped Italian parsley
1 small clove garlic, finely chopped
1 teaspoon chopped fresh sage or ¼ teaspoon leaf sage, crumbled
1 teaspoon grated lemon rind

1. Combine the flour, salt, and pepper in a plastic bag. Add the veal shank and toss to coat.

2. In a heavy casserole or Dutch oven heat the oil and brown the shank on all sides. Remove and set aside.

3. Add the garlic, onion, and carrot and sauté 2 to 3 minutes or until tender but not browned.

4. Add white wine, tomato sauce, and water. Bring to a boil; return shank, cover and simmer 45 minutes. Turn the shank, cover, and simmer 45 minutes longer or until tender.

5. Meanwhile, combine the parsley, garlic, sage, and lemon rind. Remove the meat from the shank, return to the casserole, and sprinkle with the parsley mixture.

Note: This is a great dish to make on a weekend and keep in the refrigerator to reheat one night during the week.

STUFFED VEALBURGERS

As fast as hamburgers but so much tastier. For dinner in less than half an hour serve with Parsleyed Green Beans (page 132), noodles, spinach salad, Italian macaroons and tortoni.

½ pound ground veal
¼ cup soft fresh bread crumbs
1 tablespoon finely chopped onion
1 teaspoon snipped fresh dillweed or ¼ teaspoon dried
Salt and pepper
1 ounce Chevre (goat cheese)
1 tablespoon vegetable oil
2 tablespoons butter or margarine
2 teaspoons lemon juice
2 tablespoons sour cream or plain yogurt
Paprika

1. In a medium-size bowl combine the veal, crumbs, onion, dill, salt, and pepper. Divide into 8 equal amounts and flatten into patties. Spread goat cheese over 4 patties; cover with remaining patties, pressing edges to seal.

2. Heat the oil and 1 tablespoon of the butter in a medium-size skillet. Cook patties on one side for 3 minutes; turn and cook on other side 4 minutes or until done. Transfer to heated plate.

3. Add remaining tablespoon butter and lemon juice to skillet. Bring to a boil; remove from heat and stir in sour cream; pour over patties. Sprinkle with paprika.

BRATWURST IN BEER

For dinner in 30 minutes, serve with boiled red-skinned potatoes, Braised Cabbage with Caraway Seeds (page 134) or sauer-
kraut, and pears with Gorgonzola cheese.

4 bratwurst or veal sausages
Flour
2 tablespoons butter or margarine
½ cup ale or beer
Pepper

1. Place sausages in a single layer in a skillet; cover with cold
water. Bring to a boil; reduce heat and simmer, covered, 15 minutes.

2. Remove sausages and dry on paper towel; roll in flour. Heat
the butter in a skillet and brown sausages slowly on all sides. Remove to warm plates.

3. Add beer to skillet and bring to boiling while scraping up
browned-on bits. Boil until reduced and slightly thickened. Season
with pepper. Pour over sausages.

MEATLESS MAIN DISHES

CURRIED VEGETABLES

At least once a week I have a craving for a vegetarian meal and this dish is a favorite. It goes well with Spinach, Mushroom and Feta Salad (page 167), crusty bread, and Bread Pudding with Whiskey Sauce (page 211) for dessert, if you have time to make it ahead. Another dinner in less than 30 minutes.

1 tablespoon vegetable oil
1 medium-size onion, finely chopped
1 clove garlic, finely chopped
1 stalk celery, sliced on the bias
1 carrot, sliced on the bias
1 medium-size potato, diced
1 tablespoon flour
2 teaspoons curry powder, or to taste
½ teaspoon ground ginger
½ teaspoon turmeric
1⅓ cups water or vegetable broth
2 plum tomatoes, skinned and diced
Salt and pepper
2 tablespoons chopped fresh cilantro or Italian parsley

1. Heat the oil in a medium-size heavy saucepan and sauté the onion and garlic until tender but not browned. Add the celery, carrot, and potato and cook, stirring often, 2 to 3 minutes.

2. Sprinkle with flour, curry powder, ginger, and turmeric and cook, stirring, 2 minutes. Gradually stir in the water and bring to a boil.

3. Add the tomatoes, salt, and pepper. Cover and simmer 20 minutes or until the potatoes are cooked. Sprinkle with cilantro.

ZUCCHINI FRITTATA

A vegetarian main dish that's ready in 15 minutes and likely to become a favorite for lunch, brunch, and dinner. For a full meal, add Spinach, Mushroom and Feta Salad (page 167), and fresh fruit compote for dessert.

1 tablespoon vegetable oil
1 small onion, finely chopped
1 small clove garlic, finely chopped
2 small zucchini (about 4 ounces each), thinly sliced
1 tablespoon chopped fresh basil or ½ teaspoon leaf, crumbled
¼ teaspoon leaf oregano, crumbled
4 eggs, lightly beaten
Salt and pepper
2 tablespoons freshly grated Parmesan cheese

1. In a 7- to 8-inch skillet with heatproof handle heat the oil and sauté the onion and garlic until tender but not browned.

2. Add the zucchini and cook, stirring, until zucchini is crisp-tender. Add the basil and oregano to the eggs; season with salt and pepper and pour over vegetables in the skillet.

3. Set the skillet over medium heat for 1 minute; reduce heat to low and cook until almost set in the center. Sprinkle with Parmesan and slide frittata under a preheated broiler just to melt and brown the cheese.

FRENCH PIZZA

This recipe came from a French chef who uses a pastry crust instead of bread dough. Only make it when local tomatoes are at the peak of harvest, and there is fresh basil available. Serve with French bread and a salad.

Basic pastry for 7- to 8-inch bottom crust
1 tablespoon Dijon mustard
3 to 4 vine-ripened tomatoes, peeled and sliced
1 cup grated Jarlsberg or Swiss cheese
Salt and pepper
3 fresh basil leaves, chopped
2 tablespoons chopped fresh parsley
1 tablespoon snipped fresh chives

1. Preheat oven or toaster oven to 425 degrees.

2. Make the pastry and fit into a 7- or 8-inch pie plate. Prick all over; freeze 15 minutes. Bake 8 minutes. Remove from oven and paint with mustard. Bake 2 minutes longer.

3. Remove from oven and cool. Reduce oven heat to 375 degrees.

4. Layer tomato slices and cheese in pie shell, sprinkling each layer with salt and pepper, ending with tomatoes. Sprinkle the basil, parsley, and chives over the top and bake 20 minutes or until cheese is melted and tomatoes are soft.

CRUSTLESS ZUCCHINI QUICHE

in Appetizers

also makes a great meatless luncheon dish

LINGUINE PRIMAVERA

This is a pretty-looking and delicious-tasting vegetarian main dish that I serve with sliced tomato and fresh basil salad in the summer or with a tossed green salad in winter and Frozen Chocolate Dessert (page 208).

*1 individual stalk broccoli, flowerets broken up and stalk
    saved for soup (see page 16)*
1 small zucchini, cubed
6 spears asparagus (if in season), cut into thirds
1 tablespoon vegetable oil
1 clove garlic, finely chopped
¼ pound mushrooms, sliced
*¼ teaspoon leaf basil, crumbled, or 2 tablespoons chopped
    fresh*
Salt and pepper
⅛ teaspoon red pepper flakes
¼ cup half-and-half or heavy cream
¼ cup freshly grated Parmesan cheese
8 ounces linguine

1. Steam broccoli flowerets 3 minutes; plunge into ice water; drain. Steam zucchini 2 minutes; plunge into ice water; drain. Steam the asparagus pieces 3 minutes; plunge into ice water; drain.

2. In a small skillet heat the oil and sauté the garlic and mushrooms 2 to 4 minutes. Add basil, salt, pepper, red pepper flakes, cream, and cheese.

3. Cook the linguine in 4 quarts boiling water for about 7 to 8 minutes or until it is *al dente* (cooked but not soft). Drain and return to saucepan. Reheat sauce in skillet; add vegetables to sauce to heat. Pour entire mixture over linguine and toss to mix. Serve immediately with more Parmesan cheese.

ELBOW MACARONI WITH CHEESE SAUCE

This is not your standard macaroni coated with yellow glue, but a divine three-cheese sauce that bathes the pasta for delicious eating. Serve crusty bread and a hearty tossed salad full of color and Flambéed Bananas (page 200) for dessert.

3 tablespoons finely shredded Fontina cheese
3 tablespoons crumbled blue cheese
1½ ounces cream cheese (half a 3-ounce package), softened
2 tablespoons olive oil
½ teaspoon leaf basil, crumbled
¼ cup chopped fresh parsley
4 scallions, sliced
¼ cup half-and-half or heavy cream
8 ounces elbow macaroni

1. In a small bowl combine the Fontina, blue, and cream cheeses, oil, basil, parsley, scallions, and cream. Mix well with a wooden spoon.

2. Cook the macaroni according to package directions until it is *al dente* (cooked but not soft), about 8 minutes. Drain and return to hot pan. Stir in the cheese mixture and toss to coat. Serve at once with freshly grated Parmesan cheese.

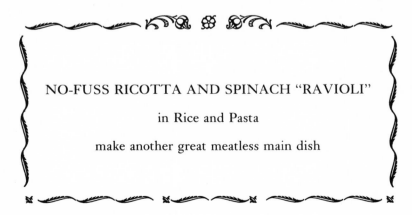

NO-FUSS RICOTTA AND SPINACH "RAVIOLI"

in Rice and Pasta

make another great meatless main dish

CHEESE-STUFFED SHELLS

X ★ ■

Serve with a mixed green salad, crusty bread if you wish, and Frozen Orange Mousse (page 202) for dessert. If you have the tomato sauce on hand and the dessert in the freezer, the meal can be on the table in 30 minutes.

1 tablespoon chopped fresh parsley
3 tablespoon freshly grated Parmesan cheese
2 tablespoons shredded mozzarella
2 tablespoons crumbled blue cheese or grated Fontina or
  Swiss cheese
2 tablespoons ricotta cheese
1 to 2 tablespoons milk or heavy cream
Pepper
1 cup Well-Seasoned Tomato Sauce (page 187) or spaghetti
  sauce
4 ounces large macaroni shells (10 to 12)

1. In a small bowl combine the parsley, 2 tablespoons of the Parmesan, mozzarella, blue or Fontina or Swiss cheese, ricotta, and enough milk to make a moldable mixture. Season with pepper.

2. Preheat oven or toaster oven to 350 degrees. Spread a thin layer of tomato sauce over the bottom of a 9×9×2-inch dish or in 2 individual au gratin dishes.

3. Cook the shells according to label directions but only until *al dente* (cooked but not soft), about 10 minutes. Drain and plunge into cold water; drain quickly.

4. Fill shells with the cheese mixture and place on top of tomato sauce in dish; pour remaining tomato sauce over shells; sprinkle with remaining Parmesan cheese and bake for 15 to 20 minutes or until bubbly hot.

Note: To use the whole box of shells (12 ounces), triple the recipe and eat one-third immediately and freeze the remaining shells in two batches. Thaw overnight and reheat in a preheated 375-degree oven for 30 minutes or until bubbly hot.

BEAN TAMALE PIE
✕ ■

I often double or triple this recipe because the individual pies freeze well and are handy to have for a quick meal with nachos, a green salad, and fresh fruit.

1 tablespoon vegetable oil
1 small onion, finely chopped
1 small clove garlic, finely chopped
1 tablespoon chili powder
¼ teaspoon ground cumin
1 tablespoon chopped chilies
1 can (16 ounces) tomatoes, drained and chopped
Salt and pepper
½ cup corn kernels, fresh, frozen, or canned
¾ cup Refried Beans (see page 192) or canned
½ cup yellow cornmeal
½ cup cold water
1 cup boiling water
Salt
1 tablespoon lard or margarine
½ cup shredded Montery Jack cheese

1. In a small skillet heat the oil and sauté the onion and garlic until soft but not browned. Add chili powder, cumin and chilies; cook, stirring, 1 minute.

2. Add tomatoes, salt, and pepper to skillet and cook uncovered over medium-high heat until sauce has thickened, about 10 minutes. Stir in corn and refried beans.

3. In a medium-size saucepan combine the cornmeal and cold water. Gradually stir in the boiling water, add salt and lard and bring to a boil; reduce heat and cook, stirring, until mixture thickens, about 10 minutes. Preheat toaster oven or oven to 350 degrees.

4. Line two individual au gratin dishes with just over half the cornmeal mixture; fill dishes with bean and corn mixture; top with remaining cornmeal mixture, spreading it to cover bean mixture. Sprinkle with cheese and bake for 25 minutes or until lightly browned and set.

VEGETABLES

RIBBONED ASPARAGUS

The fresh asparagus season is short, at least when it is at reasonable prices, so it is always good to discover a new way to fix it.

12 medium-size asparagus spears
½ cup plain yogurt or sour cream
¼ cup soft bread crumbs
1 tablespoon melted butter
2 tablespoons freshly grated Parmesan cheese
1 tablespoon chopped fresh parsley

1. Break off woody stems from asparagus where they break easily. Peel stems only if they are woody. Wash well.

2. Place spears in a large skillet and add boiling water to cover. Bring to a boil; cover and cook 5 to 6 minutes or until crisp-tender.

3. Drain on paper towels. Place in a broiler-proof serving dish; spoon a ribbon of yogurt over the middle; combine bread crumbs, butter, Parmesan cheese, and parsley and spoon over yogurt. Brown quickly under a preheated broiler.

Note: Cook extra asparagus at the same time; cool quickly in ice water; marinate in Vinaigrette Dressing (page 171) overnight and serve as an appetizer or salad. Or slice and add to scrambled eggs.

ASPARAGUS MIMOSA

At the peak of the fresh asparagus season, I often serve a hearty pea soup, Asparagus Mimosa with crusty bread and Viennese Apple Soufflé (page 199) for dessert.

1 pound (12 to 16 stalks) fresh asparagus
⅓ cup butter, melted
Salt and pepper
2 teaspoons lemon juice
2 tablespoons chopped fresh parsley
2 hard cooked eggs, finely chopped

1. Break the asparagus stalks at the natural point where the tough part meets the tender. If stalks are woody, trim with a potato peeler. Wash well to remove sand.

2. Place in a skillet with boiling water to cover. Cover pan and boil for 5 to 6 minutes, depending on thickness of stalks.

3. Meanwhile, mix the butter with the salt, pepper, lemon juice, and parsley; pour over asparagus; sprinkle with egg.

STIR-FRIED ASPARAGUS AND SNOW PEAS

It seems that when the first asparagus appears in the market, good quality fresh snow peas show up too. This is a great combination to serve with fish or poultry.

1 tablespoon vegetable oil
1 small clove garlic, finely chopped
1 teaspoon finely chopped fresh ginger root
6 asparagus spears, trimmed and cut into 1-inch lengths on the bias.
3 ounces fresh snow peas, trimmed
2 tablespoons light soy sauce
1 tablespoon water

1. In a wok or skillet heat the oil and sauté the garlic until tender. Add the ginger root, asparagus, and snow peas and stir-fry 2 minutes.

2. Add the soy sauce and water; cover and simmer 2 minutes.

SAUTÉED AVOCADO

Heating avocado brings out a slightly different flavor. The important thing is not to overheat or the taste will become bitter. An unusual side dish to serve with chicken or chili.

1 ripe avocado, peeled
2 tablespoons lemon juice
1 egg, lightly beaten
½ cup unflavored dry bread crumbs
4 tablespoons butter or margarine
1 teaspoon ground cumin

1. Cut avocado in half across; with the point of a knife remove the pit. Cut each half into 4 slices; dip slices in lemon juice.

2. Dip slices into beaten egg and then into bread crumbs placed on wax paper; pat to coat well; repeat if necessary.

3. Heat the butter and cumin in skillet; sauté the avocado slices quickly until golden on both sides.

PARSLEYED GREEN BEANS

◉

Always cook green beans this way and they will remain crisp and ready to use either hot or cold.

½ pound small whole green beans, trimmed
3 tablespoons butter or margarine
2 tablespoons finely chopped fresh parsley
Salt and pepper
½ teaspon ground nutmeg

1. Bring 2 quarts water to a rapid boil. Add beans and cook, uncovered, over high heat until crisp-tender, 5 to 8 minutes depending on freshness and size of the beans.

2. Drain beans in a colander and rinse under cold water. Dry on paper towel. Beans can now be set aside until ready to serve or marinated in Vinaigrette Dressing (page 171) for a salad.

3. When ready to serve, heat butter in a large skillet. Add beans and stir to coat. When beans are heated through, add parsley, salt, pepper, and nutmeg. Serve immediately.

GREEN BEANS WITH CAPERS

Cook the beans ahead; cool quickly in ice water; reheat a few minutes before serving.

½ pound small whole green beans, trimmed
2 tablespoons vegetable oil
1 small clove garlic, finely chopped
Pepper
1 tablespoon drained capers
1 tablespoon chopped fresh parsley

1. Place beans in a medium-size saucepan; add boiling water to come three-quarters of the way up the beans. Bring to a boil; cover and cook over high heat 5 to 8 minutes or until crisp-tender.

2. Drain in a colander and rinse under cold water until cool; drain on paper towels. Set aside until ready to serve.

3. When ready to serve, heat the oil in a medium-size skillet; add garlic and sauté over medium heat 1 minute. Add beans and toss. Season with pepper.

4. Stir in capers and parsley and reheat.

Note: If your store does not carry loose produce for you to weigh out the amount you need, ask for the size package you want.

BROCCOLI PUREE

Serve with broiled or baked fish, chicken, or roast meats.

3 cups broccoli flowerets (about half a bunch)
2 tablespoons butter or margarine
1 small bunch scallions with some green part, coarsely
*   chopped*
Salt and pepper
Dash nutmeg

1. Steam the flowerets, or boil in water, covered, until tender. Meanwhile, heat the butter in a small skillet and sauté the scallions 3 minutes.

2. Place broccoli, scallions, salt, pepper, and nutmeg in the container of a food processor. Whirl until smooth. Return to a clean pan and reheat.

Note: Double the recipe and freeze in a boil-in-the-bag. Use the stems in Broccoli Soup (page 16), or slivered in a stir-fry. Or, use the other 3 cups of flowerets in marinated vegetables, crudités, or in a stir-fry.

BRAISED CABBAGE WITH
CARAWAY SEEDS

IIIII

This is a good way to use up half a cabbage left after making cole slaw. Serve it with ham, pork, or smoked garlic sausage.

½ small green cabbage (about 8 ounces)
1 small tart apple, peeled and quartered, cored, and diced
2 tablespoons butter or margarine
¼ cup chicken broth or water
Salt and pepper
¼ teaspoon caraway seeds

1. Shred the cabbage and mix with the apple. In a medium-size saucepan, heat the butter. Add cabbage mixture and sauté 5 minutes, stirring often.

2. Add broth, salt, pepper, and caraway seeds. Bring to a boil; cover and simmer until cabbage is wilted, about 4 minutes.

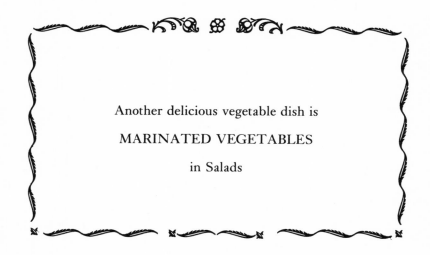

Another delicious vegetable dish is

MARINATED VEGETABLES

in Salads

CANNELLINI CASSEROLE

×

This dish is delightful with Roast Leg of Lamb (page 104) or Roast Cornish Game Hen (page 54). Double the recipe for an informal supper main dish.

2 small red-skinned potatoes, thickly sliced
½ pound eggplant (½ medium-size), peeled and diced
1 small zucchini, sliced
1 large tomato, peeled, seeded, and chopped
1 medium-size onion, finely chopped
1 tablespoon chopped parsley
1 clove garlic, finely chopped
¼ cup olive or vegetable oil
Salt and pepper
2 teaspoons chopped fresh basil or ½ teaspoon leaf, crumbled
2 teaspoons chopped fresh oregano or ¼ teaspoon leaf, crumbled
1 can (20 ounces) white kidney or cannellini beans

1. In a small, heavy, flameproof casserole layer the potatoes, eggplant, zucchini, tomato, and onion. Preheat oven to 350 degrees.

2. In a small bowl combine the parsley, garlic, oil, salt, pepper, basil, and oregano. Mix well; pour over vegetables.

3. Bring mixture to a boil, cover tightly, and bake for 45 minutes. Remove cover, add beans, and bake uncovered 30 minutes.

CELERY STICKS

Use the cooking liquid in soup or sauce or as a poaching liquid for fish or chicken.

4 large stalks celery, cut into sticks 2½ inches long by ¼-inch
  wide
1 cup chicken broth
2 tablespoons lemon juice
1 sweet green or red pepper
2 tablespoons butter, melted
Salt and pepper
1 tablespoon chopped fresh parsley

1. Tie celery sticks into two bundles with string and place in a medium-size saucepan. Add the broth and lemon juice; bring to a boil; cover and cook for 6 minutes or until crisp-tender. Drain and reserve liquid for another use.

2. Meanwhile, cut the pepper in half crosswise, and cut 2 nicely shaped rings. Place rings in a small saucepan; cover with cold water; bring to a boil; boil 1 minute. Drain and plunge rings into ice water. Preheat oven or toaster oven to 350 degrees.

3. Remove strings from celery and fit each bundle into a pepper ring. Place in a baking dish and pour butter over. Season with salt and pepper and heat in oven for 10 to 15 minutes. Sprinkle with parsley.

Note: This method of blanching green pepper keeps the green color while making it tender and great for garnishes. Use remaining raw pepper in slaw or salads.

EGGPLANT PARMIGIANA
✕ ☀

5 Serve with meats, fish, and poultry as a side dish. With a tossed green salad and crusty bread, it's a lunch or supper dish.

½ pound eggplant, cut into 4 slices (¼ inch thick) and peeled
2 tablespoons vegetable oil
1¼ cups Well-Seasoned Tomato Sauce (page 187)
3 ounces mozzarella cheese, thinly sliced
2 tablespoons freshly grated Parmesan cheese

1. Sauté the eggplant slices in the oil in a heavy skillet over low heat until tender, turning 2 to 3 times.

2. Preheat oven or toaster oven to 400 degrees.

3. In a small baking dish put 1/2 cup of the tomato sauce. Alternate slices of eggplant and mozzarella on top of the sauce. Pour over remaining tomato sauce; sprinkle with Parmesan cheese. Bake for 15 minutes.

Note: The smallest eggplant available is often 1 pound, so either double the recipe, or use half for the recipe above and the remainder in Ratatouille (page 146) or the following recipe, Sautéed Eggplant with Garlic. The recipe can be made ahead up to final baking, held refrigerated; increase baking time by 5 minutes.

Another favorite vegetable recipe is

CURRIED VEGETABLES

in meatless Main Dishes

SAUTÉED EGGPLANT WITH GARLIC

Eggplant is a good accompaniment for veal or chicken.

½ pound eggplant
2 teaspoons salt
3 tablespoons vegetable oil
1 large clove garlic, finely chopped
Pepper
2 tablespoons tomato paste
1 tablespoon chopped fresh basil or 1 teaspoon leaf, crum-
    bled
2 tablespoons chopped fresh parsley

1. Peel eggplant and cut into ½-inch dice. Place cubes in a colander; sprinkle with salt and let stand 30 minutes.

2. Rinse the eggplant well and dry on paper towels. Heat 2 tablespoons of the oil in a medium-size skillet; add garlic and sauté over medium-low heat about 1 minute or until golden. Do not burn.

3. Add the eggplant cubes and toss in the oil. Sauté the eggplant, adding the remaining tablespoon of oil, and stirring until lightly browned.

4. Season with pepper. Mix together the tomato paste and 2 tablespoons water and add to the skillet. Bring to a boil. Add basil, stir, cover, and simmer 20 minutes or until eggplant is tender.

5. Sprinkle with parsley.

BRAISED LEEKS
X ◉

Serve with roast meats or poultry.

2 medium-size leeks, trimmed and washed well, cutting
    down into the green part to get out the dirt
1 can (13¾ ounces) chicken broth
Pepper

1. Place leeks in a medium-size skillet. Add chicken broth and pepper. Cover; bring to a boil and simmer 10 minutes.

2. With tongs, turn leeks over. Cover and simmer 15 minutes longer or until leeks are tender.

Note: Use the two leeks remaining in the bunch for Potato and Leek Soup (page 25). Or, double the recipe above, eat 2 leeks warm as a vegetable, and drain remaining 2; place in a glass dish, pour over Vinaigrette Dressing (page 171), refrigerate, and serve as an appetizer or salad. Use cooking broth in soup, stew, or sauce.

LIMA BEANS IN CREAM AND CHIVES

One of my favorite ways to fix limas whether you start with fresh or frozen, and delicious with ham, poultry and pork.

1 package (10 ounces) frozen lima beans or 2 cups fresh
¼ cup chicken broth
¼ cup half-and-half or light cream
Pepper
2 tablespoons snipped fresh chives or ½ teaspoon freeze-
dried

1. Combine lima beans, broth, and cream in a heavy saucepan. Bring to a boil; cover and cook over medium heat until limas are just tender, about 5 minutes. Uncover pan and cook until beans are fully tender and liquid has thickened.

2. Sprinkle with pepper and chives and serve at once.

AMBER ONION SLICES

A great vegetable to serve with hamburger, meat loaf, or chops.

1 large sweet Spanish onion
1 tablespoon butter or margarine
2 tablespoons tomato juice or chili sauce
2 tablespoons honey
½ teaspoon paprika
Salt

1. Preheat oven or toaster oven to 350 degrees.
2. Peel onion and cut into 4 thick slices. Place in one layer in baking dish.
3. Combine butter, tomato juice, honey, paprika, and salt in a small saucepan and heat, stirring, until well blended. Pour over onion slices; cover dish and bake for 40 minutes or until onions are tender and glazed.

CARROT PARSNIP PUREE

I guarantee that the non-parsnip-lover will ask for more of this tasty, colorful combination. I always use the entire market unit of each vegetable as long as I am going to the trouble to make it. The recipe makes 6 cups and I know two people can eat 1½ cups and I freeze the remainder in boil-in-the-bags for three other meals.

1 pound carrots, scraped and sliced
1 pound parsnips, scraped and sliced
1 small onion, quartered
4 large sprigs parsley
3 tablespoons butter or margarine
Salt and pepper

1. Place carrots and parsnips in a large saucepan with water barely to cover. Bring to a boil; cover and simmer until tender, about 15 minutes.

2. Drain the vegetables very well.

3. Place onion and parsley in the container of an electric blender or food processor and whirl or process until very fine.

4. Add hot vegetables and butter and whirl or process until very smooth. Season with salt and pepper.

PUREE OF PEAS

Purees can be done ahead of time, using the food processor, or electric blender, and reheated. For a fancy presentation pipe the mixture from a pastry bag fitted with a star tip and surround with julienne strips of cooked carrot.

1 package (10 ounces) frozen tiny peas
2 tablespoons butter or margarine
2 to 3 tablespoons half-and-half or heavy cream
Salt and pepper
¼ teaspoon ground nutmeg

1. Cook peas until very tender following label directions. Drain well and turn into the container of an electric blender or food processor.

2. Add butter, half-and-half, salt, pepper, and nutmeg and whirl or process until smooth.

WINTER PETITS POIS

With this recipe (and a few out-of-season strawberries), it is possible to close your eyes and think of summer.

2 tablespoons butter
1 shallot, finely chopped
1 package (10 ounces) frozen tiny peas
Salt and pepper
½ teaspoon sugar
2 large Boston lettuce leaves
2 tablespoons chopped fresh parsley

1. Heat the butter in a medium-size saucepan and sauté the shallot for 2 minutes.

2. Add the peas, salt, pepper, sugar, lettuce leaves, and 2 tablespoons hot water. Cover and bring to a boil. Break up the peas; cover and simmer 3 minutes or until peas are thawed. Uncover; remove lettuce leaves and discard; evaporate excess liquid by boiling 1 minute. Sprinkle with parsley.

Note: If you find that one 10-ounce package of frozen peas is too much, add leftovers to soup, stew, or salad. Or, collect in the freezer for vegetable soup or to add to a chicken pot pie.

RICE AND PEAS VENETIAN STYLE

Great with veal or chicken.

3 tablespoons butter
1 small onion, finely chopped
¾ cup long-grain rice
1 can (13¾ ounces) chicken broth
½ package (10 ounces) frozen tiny peas
2 tablespoons grated Parmesan cheese
Salt and pepper

1. In a medium-size saucepan heat the butter and sauté the onion until tender but not browned. Add rice and cook, stirring, 2 to 3 minutes or until rice is opaque.

2. Add chicken broth. Bring to a boil; cover and simmer 20 minutes or until rice has absorbed the broth and is tender. Add water if necessary.

3. Add peas, Parmesan cheese, salt, and pepper; reheat.

SUMMER GARDEN PEAS

Make a supper out of a big bowl of peas with bread, cheese and strawberry shortcake . . . on the porch, terrace, or patio. Great eating!

1½ to 2 pounds peas in the pod
6 to 8 Boston lettuce leaves
1 shallot, finely chopped
4 tablespoons (½ stick) butter
3 tablespoons half-and-half
Salt and pepper

1. Shell the peas. Place the lettuce leaves in the bottom of a medium-size saucepan. Pour peas on top; sprinkle with shallot and dot with butter.

2. Cover and cook over medium-high heat until peas are tender, about 7 to 10 minutes.

3. Stir in half-and-half; season with salt and pepper. Serve with lettuce and juices in heated bowls.

SCALLOPED POTATOES

Potato lovers will be able to eat a whole dish of these or, if you prefer one dish to serve two, with other vegetables, refrigerate the second dish for another night. It will keep four to five days.

2 medium-size potatoes (½ pound each), pared and thinly
  sliced
1 small onion, finely chopped
2 teaspoons flour
Salt and pepper
1 ½ to 1 ¾ cups milk or light cream
3 tablespoons butter or margarine
2 tablespoons freshly grated Parmesan cheese

1. Butter two individual oval au gratin dishes (8×4 inches, 1½ to 2 cups capacity). Preheat oven or toaster oven to 350 degrees.

2. Place half the potatoes in the 2 dishes. Scatter the onion over; sprinkle each with flour, salt, and pepper.

3. Heat the milk to simmer (little bubbles appear around the edge of the pan). Place remaining potato slices in the dishes. Pour over the milk; dot with butter and sprinkle with cheese. Bake for 45 to 60 minutes or until potatoes are tender.

Another delicious vegetable dish is

MARINATED VEGETABLES

in Salads

TWICE-BAKED HERB-STUFFED POTATOES

Make ahead up to the second baking.

2 Russet baking potatoes
¼ cup light cream or milk, warmed
4 tablespoons (½ stick) butter, melted
2 tablespoons snipped fresh chives or 1 teaspoon freeze-dried
1 tablespoon chopped fresh parsley
Salt and pepper
1 tablespoon grated Parmesan cheese

1. Preheat oven or toaster oven to 425 degrees. Scrub, rinse, dry, and prick potatoes and place directly on oven rack. Bake 1 hour or until tender. Remove and cool slightly.

2. Cut about ⅓ of tops off and scoop out flesh into the small bowl of an electric mixer. Add cream, butter, chives, parsley, salt, and pepper. Beat on low speed until smooth.

3. Fill potato shell with herb mixture; sprinkle with Parmesan and bake for 15 minutes until hot and lightly browned.

Note: If potatoes are made ahead, they will take 20 to 25 minutes to reheat.

RATATOUILLE
× ■

This is a scaled-down version of the ratatouille I make at the peak of the fresh tomato season, but it provides enough for two meals as a side dish and freezes well in boilable bags.

1 small eggplant (about 1 pound)
¼ cup vegetable oil*
1 small sweet green pepper, cored, seeded, and cut into strips
1 small sweet red pepper, cored, seeded and cut into strips
1 small zucchini, sliced
1 medium-size onion, sliced thinly
1 clove garlic, finely chopped
1 can (8 ounces) stewed tomatoes
Salt and pepper
2 tablespoons chopped fresh parsley

1. Peel, slice, and cube the eggplant. Heat 2 tablespoons of the oil in a large skillet and sauté the eggplant until almost tender. Remove with a slotted spoon to a bowl.

2. Add one of the remaining tablespoons of oil to skillet and sauté the peppers and zucchini until almost tender. Remove to bowl.

3. Add remaining oil and sauté the onion and garlic until tender. Pour in tomatoes and bring to a boil, scraping up the browned-on bits. Return vegetables to skillet and add salt and pepper. Bring to a boil; cover and simmer 15 minutes. Sprinkle with parsley.

* To reduce the oil by a half, broil the eggplant slices until tender and then dice.

WILTED SPINACH

Serve with chops, chicken, or Chinese dishes.

1 tablespoon vegetable oil
1 clove garlic, finely chopped
8 small mushrooms (about 4 ounces), sliced
4 thin slices fresh ginger root or ¼ teaspoon ground ginger
6 ounces fresh spinach leaves or ½ polybag (10 ounces),
    washed, trimmed, and dried
Salt and pepper

1. Heat the oil in a wok or heavy skillet. Stir-fry the garlic, mushrooms, and ginger root 3 minutes.
2. Add the spinach, salt, and pepper and cook very briefly, just until the spinach is wilted.

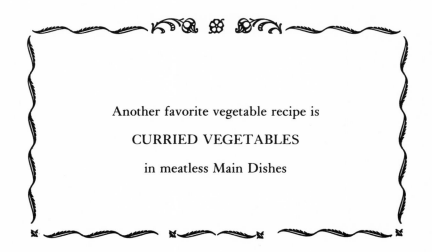

Another favorite vegetable recipe is

CURRIED VEGETABLES

in meatless Main Dishes

BRUSSELS SPROUTS AND CHESTNUTS

This is a classic recipe for Thanksgiving and Christmas dinners. If it is a favorite, prepare extra chestnuts and freeze them to enjoy the dish all winter long.

6 chestnuts
8 to 10 ounces fresh Brussels sprouts or 1 package frozen (10 ounces)
3 tablespoons butter
Salt and pepper

1. With a sharp knife, make an *X* in the flat side of each chestnut. Put them in a small saucepan and cover with cold water. Bring to a boil and boil gently 15 minutes. Remove from hot water one at a time and peel off outer and inner skins with a knife. Chestnuts are ready to use in this and other recipes.

2. Trim bottom and outer leaves from sprouts. Make an *X* in the bottom of the stem. Add to a medium-size saucepan of boiling water; cover and boil 5 to 8 minutes, depending on size, or until crisp-tender. Or, cook frozen sprouts according to label directions. Drain; rinse under cold water.

3. Heat butter in a medium-size skillet. Add sprouts and chestnuts, salt and pepper and toss over low heat until hot.

BAKED BUTTERNUT SQUASH

The squash will cook alongside Cornish game hens and be ready in about the same time.

1 small butternut, hubbard, or acorn squash (about 1 pound)
2 tablespoons butter or margarine, melted
¼ cup light brown sugar
¼ teaspoon ground cinnamon
⅛ teaspoon ground nutmeg

1. Preheat oven or toaster oven to 350 degrees.

2. Halve the squash lengthwise and remove seeds and membranes. Place in a shallow baking dish. Combine butter, sugar, cinnamon, and nutmeg and divide between cavities of squash.

3. Add ¼-inch depth of hot water to dish and bake for 50 minutes or until squash is tender.

SWEET POTATO PATTIES

They go well with ham, poultry, and pork.

2 medium-size sweet potatoes
3 tablespoons butter or margarine
½ teaspoon ground ginger
Salt and pepper
3 tablespoons finely ground walnuts

1. Preheat oven or toaster oven to 400 degrees.

2. Bake potatoes 45 minutes or until tender. Split and scoop out the flesh into a food mill or potato ricer. Press through into a bowl.

3. Beat in 1 tablespoon of the butter, the ginger, salt, and pepper. Shape into 4 patties. Roll in nuts. Place on plate and chill in the freezer for 20 minutes. Heat remaining butter in a skillet and sauté patties on both sides until crispy and hot. Nuts burn easily, so cook over medium heat.

WHITE TURNIP AND CARROT

A colorful medley that is good with roasts of meat and poultry and with fish. Add to a curry or chicken pot pie.

1 small white turnip (8 ounces), peeled and cut into ¼-inch dice
4 carrots (8 ounces), scraped and cut into ¼-inch dice
1½ tablespoons butter
1½ teaspoons chopped fresh chives or ½ teaspoon freeze-dried
Salt and pepper

1. Place the turnip and carrot in a medium-size saucepan. Add water to come halfway up the vegetables. Bring to a boil; partially cover and simmer 10 minutes or until the vegetables are crisp-tender. Drain if necessary.

2. Add the butter, chives, salt, and pepper and toss.

ZUCCHINI LIMONE

One more way to enjoy summer's bounty of zucchini.

2 small zucchini (about ½ pound)
2 tablespoons olive oil
Pepper
2 tablespoons lemon juice
1 tablespoon drained capers
1 tablespoon chopped fresh parsley

1. Cut the zucchini into thin slices; place in a medium-size skillet; cover with boiling water. Bring to a boil; cover and cook 3 to 5 minutes or until crisp-tender. Drain and dry on paper towels.

2. Place zucchini in two layers in a glass or ceramic serving dish. Combine oil, pepper, lemon juice, and capers and pour over zucchini. Toss to coat. Serve at room temperature or refrigerate overnight and let come to room temperature before serving. Sprinkle with parsley.

STIR-FRIED VEGETABLES

Vary the mix of vegetables according to the season and availability. Delicious with broiled flank steak (page 89), broiled fish, or chicken.

3 stalks celery, cut on the bias into 2-inch pieces
1 small onion, cut into eighths
1 sweet red pepper, cored, seeded, and chunked
6 asparagus spears, cut on the bias into 2-inch pieces
3 scallions, cut on the bias into 2-inch pieces
3 tablespoons vegetable oil
1 tablespoon soy sauce
1 tablespoon dry sherry
½ teaspoon cider vinegar
1 teaspoon cornstarch
⅛ teaspoon red pepper flakes (optional)

1. Prepare all the vegetables and set them in piles near the stove.

2. Heat 2 tablespoons of the oil in a wok or skillet. Add the celery, onion, and red pepper and stir-fry over medium heat for 3 to 4 minutes.

3. Add the asparagus spears and scallions and stir-fry 3 to 4 minutes longer. In a small cup mix the soy sauce, sherry, vinegar, and cornstarch together. Stir into the wok until vegetables are coated with the sauce. Add the flakes and stir to mix.

SALADS

CHEF'S SALAD

IIIII

An alternative to the usual ham combination. Serve with hot biscuits or croissants and fruit of the season for dessert.

¾ to 1 quart washed, drained, and crisped salad greens
(Bibb, Boston, leaf or bronze lettuce)
4 scallions, chopped
1 sweet red pepper, cored, seeded, and diced
6 cherry tomatoes, halved
¼ cucumber, peeled and diced
4 radishes, sliced
⅓ cup cubed Fontina or Gruyère cheese
½ cup julienne strips cooked chicken or turkey breast
1 hard-cooked egg, sliced
Vinaigrette Dressing (page 171)

1. In a medium-size salad bowl combine the salad greens, scallions, pepper, tomatoes, cucumber, and radishes. Toss to mix.

2. Arrange cheese, chicken, and egg slices in a pattern on top of salad. Toss with dressing at table just before serving.

CHICKEN AND GRAPE SALAD

||||

This is a refreshing salad on a hot summer's day. Serve with Chilled Cucumber Soup (page 19), melba toast, and watermelon.

1½ cups cooked diced chicken (1 large breast)*
2 stalks celery, sliced
4 radishes, sliced
4 scallions, sliced
¾ cup seedless grapes, red or green, halved
2 tablespoons mayonnaise
¼ cup plain yogurt
Grated rind of 1 large orange
2 tablespoons chopped toasted almonds
Salt and pepper
Boston lettuce leaves

1. In a medium-size bowl combine chicken, celery, radishes, scallions, and grapes.

2. In a small bowl combine the mayonnaise, yogurt, rind, almonds, salt, and pepper. Stir to mix; pour over chicken mixture and chill. Serve on lettuce leaves.

* For emergencies, I keep a package of frozen cooked diced chicken in the freezer. It has 3 cups of meat but it is possible just to take out the amount you need.

BLACK-EYED PEAS SALAD

||||| ☀

Start a dinner with Cream of Celery and Blue Cheese Soup (page 17); serve sliced tomatoes with the salad and have sherbet for dessert.

⅓ cup Vinaigrette Dressing (page 171)
1 small onion, finely chopped
2 tablespoons chopped parsley
1 small clove garlic, finely chopped
½ teaspoon leaf basil, crumbled
¼ teaspoon leaf oregano, crumbled
⅛ teaspoon dry mustard
⅛ teaspoon pepper
Pinch red pepper flakes
1 package (10 ounces) frozen black-eyed peas, cooked according to package directions
1 cup cooked, cubed chicken or turkey
1 small green pepper, cored, seeded, and diced

1. Place the vinaigrette dressing in a jar with a tight-fitting cover. Add onion, parsley, garlic, basil, oregano, mustard, pepper, and red pepper flakes. Cover and shake well.

2. Place drained, hot black-eyed peas in a bowl and pour over the dressing. Stir in the chicken or turkey, cover and refrigerate several hours or overnight. Add green pepper just before serving.

CHICK-PEA AND CHEESE SALAD

Hearty enough to make a meal when teamed with soup, sandwich or rich dessert.

1 can (20 ounces) chick-peas, drained and rinsed
1 cup diced Fontina or Gruyère cheese
½ cup sliced celery
4 scallions, chopped with green part
½ sweet red pepper, cored, seeded, and diced
3 anchovy fillets, chopped, or 1 tablespoon drained capers
Vinaigrette Dressing (page 171)
2 tablespoons chopped fresh parsley

1. In a medium-size bowl combine the chick-peas, cheese, celery, scallions, pepper, and anchovy fillets.

2. Shake the dressing well and pour over enough to well moisten the salad. Chill several hours or overnight. Add parsley and more dressing if needed before serving.

RICE SALAD WITH HAM AND APPLE

and COLD RICE SALAD

in Rice and Pasta

are two other unusual salads

SMOKED TURKEY AND
CHICK-PEA SALAD

A main dish salad to put together the night before or early in the day you plan to serve it. Add crusty bread and a rich dessert like Apple Almond Tarts (page 197).

2 tablespoons olive or vegetable oil
1 tablespoon lemon juice
1 tablespoon garlic-flavored wine vinegar
⅛ teaspoon dry mustard
Salt and pepper
1 package (about 2½ ounces) smoked turkey, diced, or 1 cup
    diced Genoa salami
1 small zucchini, diced
⅓ cup diced Swiss cheese
2 tablespoons chopped fresh parsley
1 can (20 ounces) chick-peas or cannellini beans, drained
1 sweet green pepper, seeded, cored, and diced
6 scallions, sliced
Boston lettuce leaves

1. In a jar with a screw-top lid combine the oil, lemon juice, vinegar, mustard, salt, and pepper. Shake well to mix.

2. In a large bowl combine the smoked turkey, zucchini, cheese, parsley, chick-peas, green pepper, and scallions; pour over the dressing; toss to mix and refrigerate several hours or overnight. Serve on lettuce leaves.

HAM AND LIMA BEAN SALAD

A main dish salad that is best made the night before to allow the flavors to penetrate the beans. Serve with a hot or cold soup such as Potato and Leek Soup (page 25) and crusty bread.

1 package (10 ounces) baby lima beans, cooked according to label directions
2 tablespoons olive or vegetable oil
1 tablespoon lemon juice
1 tablespoon wine vinegar
1 clove garlic, crushed
½ teaspoon Italian herbs
⅛ teaspon red pepper flakes
Salt and pepper
4 scallions, chopped
½ sweet red pepper, cored, seeded, and diced
½ sweet green pepper, cored, seeded, and diced
1 stalk celery, sliced
4 ounces cooked deli ham, cut into bite-size pieces
2 tablespoons chopped fresh parsley
Boston lettuce leaves

1. Place the cooked and drained beans in a bowl. In a jar with a screw-top lid, place the oil, lemon juice, vinegar, garlic, herbs, pepper flakes, salt, and pepper and shake to mix well. Pour over the hot beans and set aside to reach room temperature.

2. Add scallions, peppers, celery, ham, and parsley; cover and refrigerate several hours or overnight. Serve on lettuce leaves.

CAESAR SALAD

Great with chops, steaks, steak Diane, and A Perfect Roast Chicken (page 53).

2 tablespoons olive oil
1 small clove garlic, crushed
½ cup small bread cubes, crusts removed
2 flat anchovy fillets
1 tablespoon lemon juice
Dash pepper
⅛ teaspoon dry mustard
⅛ teaspoon Worcestershire sauce
1 quart torn romaine lettuce leaves
1 egg yolk
2 tablespoons freshly grated Parmesan cheese

1. Place the oil and garlic in a custard cup and leave overnight.

2. Next day, discard the garlic. In a small skillet heat the oil and sauté the bread cubes until crisp and golden. Drain on paper towel.

3. When ready to serve, in a medium-size salad bowl mash the anchovies with the lemon juice, pepper, mustard, and Worcestershire.

4. Add the lettuce; toss. Add egg yolk and cheese; toss. Add the croutons and serve immediately.

COLE SLAW WITH PEPPERS
AND PICKLES

✕ ☀

This recipe can be doubled and will keep up to three days in the refrigerator if you wish to serve it twice in a week. Alternately, the other half of the cabbage can be used in Braised Cabbage with Caraway Seeds (page 134).

8 ounces green cabbage (half a small cabbage), shredded
1 small sweet red pepper, cored, seeded, and diced
¼ cup chopped sweet gherkins
1 scallion, chopped
2 tablespoons mayonnaise
3 tablespoons plain yogurt or sour cream
1 tablespoon garlic-flavored wine vinegar
½ teaspoon ground celery seeds

1. Place cabbage, pepper, gherkins, and scallion in a bowl. In a 1-cup measure combine the mayonnaise, yogurt, vinegar, and celery seed; pour over cabbage mixture and toss to mix.

2. Refrigerate, covered, several hours before serving.

RITZ CUCUMBERS

A slightly different way to treat cucumbers.

1 medium-size cucumber
½ cup water
¼ cup sugar
2 tablespoons cider vinegar
2 tablespoons vegetable oil

1. Peel cucumber if waxed; slice very thinly.

2. In a small saucepan combine water, sugar, and vinegar; bring to a boil; add cucumber slices and simmer 3 to 4 minutes.

3. Remove from heat and add oil; cool. Refrigerate several hours. Pour off accumulated liquid before serving.

ENDIVE AND BEET SALAD

Good with Roast Leg of Lamb (page 104).

1 head Belgian endive
1 can (8 ounces) julienned beets
1 tablespoon mayonnaise
3 tablespoons Vinaigrette Dressing (page 171)
1 scallion, chopped
1 tablespoon chopped fresh parsley

1. Slice the endive lengthwise, making thin julienne strips. Drain beets and dry well on paper towel.
2. Arrange endive and beets on salad plates in alternating rows. Beat together the mayonnaise and vinaigrette dressing.
3. Sprinkle scallion over salads, pour over dressing, and sprinkle with parsley.

ENDIVE AND WATERCRESS SALAD

A refreshing winter salad when both ingredients are in season.

1 head Belgian endive
½ bunch watercress
Vinaigrette Dressing (page 171)
Freshly ground pepper

1. Cut the endive lengthwise into julienne strips.
2. Wash and trim watercress and arrange on salad plates; top with endive. Sprinkle lightly with dressing and pepper. Garnish with orange or grapefruit sections, if you wish.

FRESH FRUIT SALAD

For a light summertime lunch, I serve the fruit salad in Bibb or Boston lettuce leaves with a scoop of low-fat cottage cheese on the side and pass the dressing separately. Add a bran or whole-wheat muffin and no one will look for dessert.

1 peach or nectarine
1 cup melon balls
1 cup sliced strawberries
½ cup seedless grapes
1 tablespoon sliced almonds
Honey Yogurt Dressing (page 170)

1. Dip peach in boiling water to a count of 7; peel, halve, pit, and slice into a serving bowl.
2. Add melon balls, strawberries, grapes, and almonds. Serve dressing separately.

MUSHROOM SALAD

A peppy accompaniment for sautéed veal, chicken, or turkey cutlets. (See Veal Piccata, page 111.)

1 tablespoon lemon juice
2 tablespoons Dijon mustard
Dash of salt
⅛ teaspoon pepper
Pinch leaf thyme, crumbled
2 tablespoons olive oil
¼ pound mushrooms, sliced (1 cup)
2 Boston lettuce leaves

1. In a small bowl combine the lemon juice, mustard, salt, pepper, and thyme. With a small whisk, slowly whisk in the oil to make a thick dressing.
2. Add the mushrooms; toss and serve on lettuce leaves.

PERSIMMON AND AVOCADO SALAD

Persimmon is one of the most beautiful of fall's fruits but it must be absolutely ripe, bright orange and soft to be sweet to the taste. Unripe persimmons pucker the mouth.

1 ripe persimmon
1 ripe avocado
Salad greens
Vinaigrette Dressing (page 171)

1. Peel the persimmon and slice lengthwise. Peel half the avocado and slice lengthwise. Wrap remaining half tightly with plastic wrap and store in the refrigerator. Use as soon as possible in guacamole or another salad.

2. Arrange the greens on 2 salad plates. Alternate slices of persimmon with slices of avocado. Drizzle with dressing.

AVOCADO HALVES WITH SPICY SAUCE

in Appetizers

also make a delicious separate salad course

NORMANDY POTATO SALAD

This salad goes well with barbecued meats and poultry.

½ pound new, thin-skinned potatoes
¼ cup chicken broth
¼ cup vegetable oil
2 tablespoons cider vinegar
Salt and pepper
¼ pound tiny mushrooms, sliced
2 to 3 tablespoons Vinaigrette Dressing (page 171)
½ sweet green pepper, cored, seeded, and cut into julienne
*   strips*
1 small shallot, finely chopped
2 tablespoons chopped fresh parsley

1. Boil potatoes in water to cover until barely tender. Do not peel, but chill several hours or until cold and firm.

2. Preheat oven or toaster oven to 350 degrees.

3. Slice potatoes into ¼-inch slices and layer in overlapping rows in a baking dish. Combine broth, oil, vinegar, salt, and pepper and pour over potatoes.

4. Bake for 20 minutes. Cool to room temperature. Toss mushrooms in Vinaigrette Dressing.

5. Layer potatoes and mushrooms in a salad bowl with pepper strips, shallot, and parsley. Serve at room temperature.

SPINACH, MUSHROOM, AND FETA SALAD

A pleasant combination of flavors that complements many main dishes.

½ polybag (10 ounces) spinach or ½ pound loose fresh
2 ounces mushrooms, sliced
¼ cup crumbled feta cheese
½ red onion, sliced into thin rings
1 tablespoon red wine vinegar
1 tablespoon lemon juice
1 tablespoon Dijon mustard
Salt and pepper

1. Wash and trim the spinach and dry in a spinner or on paper towels; tear into bite-size pieces into a salad bowl.

2. Add mushrooms, feta cheese, and onion rings.

3. In a jar with a tight-fitting cover combine the vinegar, lemon juice, mustard, salt, and pepper. Shake to mix.

4. Toss salad with dressing just before serving.

RICE SALAD WITH HAM AND APPLE

and COLD RICE SALAD

in Rice and Pasta

are two other unusual salads

TABBOULEH
(CRACKED WHEAT SALAD)

Only make this dish when fresh mint is available. I take it on picnics to eat with cold Fruit Stuffed Cornish Game Hens (page 57).

1 cup bulghur (cracked wheat)
½ cup boiling water
2 scallions, finely chopped
½ sweet green pepper, cored, seeded, and diced
½ stalk celery, diced
¼ cup finely chopped Italian parsley
¼ cup chopped fresh mint
1 plum tomato, skinned, seeded, and chopped
1 tablespoon lemon juice
1 tablespoon olive oil
¼ teaspoon salt
¼ teaspoon pepper

1. Place bulghur in a small bowl; pour over the boiling water and let soak 10 to 15 minutes. Drain and squeeze dry.

2. Place bulghur in a serving bowl and add scallions, green pepper, celery, parsley, mint, and tomato. Toss to mix.

3. In a screw-top jar combine lemon juice, oil, salt, and pepper. Shake to mix. Pour over bulghur mixture. Toss to mix. Chill overnight.

MARINATED VEGETABLES

A delicious salad served on lettuce, or add a can (20 ounces) of drained chick-peas and a can (3½ ounces) of tuna for a light main dish.

1 single stalk broccoli, cut into small flowerets (hold stalk
for Broccoli Soup, page 16)
1 carrot, cut into ¼-inch pennies
2 stalks celery, sliced or diced
4 ounces button mushrooms
1 small zucchini or yellow squash, cut into ¼-inch slices
4 scallions, chopped
2 tablespoons olive or vegetable oil
2 tablespoons red wine vinegar
1 clove garlic, crushed
Salt and pepper
2 tablespoons chopped fresh parsley

1. Steam the broccoli flowerets about 3 minutes or until crisp-tender; plunge into ice water; drain. Steam the carrot over the same water for 4 minutes; plunge into ice water and drain. Place broccoli and carrot in a medium-size bowl. Add celery and mushrooms.

2. Steam the zucchini over the same water for 2 minutes; plunge into ice water; drain and add to other vegetables. Add the scallions.

3. In a jar with a tight-fitting lid combine the oil, vinegar, garlic, salt, and pepper. Shake to mix.

4. Pour dressing over vegetables; toss to mix; refrigerate several hours, tossing several times. Stir in parsley.

HONEY YOGURT DRESSING

Great for fruit salads, avocados, and endive leaves.

½ cup plain yogurt
1 teaspoon lemon juice
1 tablespoon frozen orange juice concentrate, thawed
1 teaspoon grated orange rind
1 tablespoon honey
1 tablespoon toasted sesame seeds*

1. In a small bowl combine all the ingredients; mix well. Pour over fruits or pass separately.

* To toast sesame seeds, place in a small skillet and heat over low heat, shaking frequently until lightly toasted. Do not allow to burn. Cool.

CREAMY BLUE CHEESE DRESSING

This dressing is delicious on tossed greens, spinach, and endive salad, among others. It will keep a week in the refrigerator.

1 tablespoon Dijon mustard
Salt and pepper
½ egg yolk*
1 teaspoon chopped fresh parsley
½ clove garlic, finely chopped
⅓ cup olive or vegetable oil
1 tablespoon red wine vinegar
1 teaspoon lemon juice
½ container (8 ounces) plain yogurt
2 tablespoons crumbled blue cheese

1. In a small bowl combine the mustard, salt, pepper, egg yolk, parsley, and garlic. Whisk briskly to mix.

2. Slowly whisk in the oil to make a smooth, creamy mixture. Whisk in the vinegar, lemon juice, yogurt, and blue cheese.

* Double recipe to use whole yolk or add to scrambled eggs, fried rice, etc.

VINAIGRETTE DRESSING

This will keep two to three weeks in the refrigerator, so keep it on hand to use with many different salads.

⅔ cup olive or vegetable oil
¼ cup red wine vinegar
1 clove garlic, crushed.
1 shallot, finely chopped
¼ teaspoon pepper
¼ cup chopped fresh parsley
¼ teaspoon Italian herbs
1 teaspoon Dijon mustard (optional)

Place all ingredients in a jar with a screw-top cover. Shake to blend and store in the refrigerator.

RICE AND PASTA

FRIED RICE

||||

This is delicious with all stir-fried dishes, and as a side dish with grilled meats and poultry.

3 tablespoons vegetable oil
2 eggs, lightly beaten
2 scallions, cut on the bias into ½-inch pieces
2 cups cooked rice (⅔ cup raw)
⅓ cup diced cooked ham (2 deli slices), or cooked roast pork
½ can (8 ounces) water chestnuts, sliced (7 to 8)
1 tablespoon soy sauce

1. Heat 1 tablespoon oil in a wok or heavy skillet. Add the eggs and cook, stirring, until scrambled. Remove to a board. Chop.

2. Add remaining oil to the wok; add scallions and rice and stir-fry 3 minutes; add the ham, water chestnuts, chopped egg, and soy sauce. Reheat.

COLD RICE SALAD

||||| ☀

Colorful addition to cold meats and easy to take to a picnic.

⅓ cup rice, cooked according to label directions, or 1 cup cooked rice
2 tablespoons olive or vegetable oil
1 tablespoon lemon juice
1 tablespoon garlic-flavored wine vinegar
⅛ teaspon dry mustard
Salt and pepper
1 individual stalk broccoli
1 carrot, sliced
3 radishes, sliced
½ sweet red pepper, cored, seeded, and diced
4 scallions, sliced
¼ cup diced toasted almonds

1. Place the hot cooked rice in a medium-size bowl. In a screw-top jar combine oil, lemon juice, vinegar, mustard, salt, and pepper. Shake to mix. Pour over hot rice and allow to reach room temperature.

2. Break broccoli into small flowerets; keep stalk for soup (see page 16). Steam flowerets 3 minutes; drain and plunge into ice water. Steam carrots 3 minutes; drain and plunge into ice water.

3. Drain broccoli and carrot and add to rice along with radishes, pepper, and scallions. Chill several hours or overnight. Add almonds just before serving.

CONFETTI RICE

A pretty dish, quickly prepared from leftover rice.

2 tablespoons butter or margarine
1 tablespoon vegetable oil
½ sweet green pepper, cored, seeded, and diced
½ sweet red pepper, cored, seeded, and diced
½ cup frozen corn kernels, thawed
¾ cup cooked rice
Salt and pepper
2 to 3 drops liquid hot pepper seasoning
1 tablespoon chopped parsley

1. Heat the butter and oil in a medium-size skillet; sauté the peppers 2 minutes.
2. Add corn and rice and cook, stirring, until mixture is heated through. Add salt, pepper, hot pepper seasoning, and parsley.

RICE SALAD WITH HAM AND APPLE

Good with cold meats and poultry and great to take on a picnic.

½ cup long-grain rice
2 tablespoons Vinaigrette Dressing (page 171)
½ cup diced cooked ham
1 red-skinned apple, quartered, cored, and diced
1 teaspoon lemon juice
Mayonnaise
¼ cup slivered almonds

1. Cook the rice according to label directions. Place in a bowl with Vinaigrette Dressing and let stand to cool.
2. Stir in ham, apple, and lemon juice. Add enough mayonnaise to bind. Chill. Sprinkle with almonds before serving.

LEMON RICE

A nice complement for poultry and fish and Chinese dishes.

½ cup long-grain rice
2 tablespoons butter or margarine
Juice of half a lemon or to taste
Salt and pepper
1 tablespoon chopped fresh parsley

1. Place rice and butter in a small saucepan and cook, stirring, 3 minutes or until rice is translucent; add 1 cup water; bring to a boil; cover and simmer 15 minutes or until rice has absorbed the liquid.
2. Stir in lemon juice, salt, pepper, and parsley.

WILD RICE

■

I make the whole batch and freeze the extra in boil-in-the-bags in meal-size portions.

1 cup wild rice
4 cups water
1 teaspoon salt

1. Wash the rice thoroughly and place in a large heavy saucepan with water and salt. Bring to a boil; cover and simmer 45 minutes or until rice is tender but not mushy.
2. Fluff rice with a fork; cover and simmer 5 minutes longer. Drain if necessary.

SUPER MACARONI AND CHEESE

Hearty enough to serve as a main dish, it is great served with Ratatouille (page 146), a tossed green salad, and fruit for dessert. Dinner can be ready in about 45 minutes.

¾ cup elbow macaroni
1 sweet Italian sausage
2 tablespoons butter or margarine
½ small onion, finely chopped
2 tablespoons flour
¼ cup dry white wine or vermouth
¾ cup milk
¾ cup grated Swiss or Gruyère cheese
Salt and pepper

1. Cook the macaroni according to label directions, until *al dente* or almost tender, drain and reserve.

2. Remove casing from the sausage and sauté in a medium-size saucepan, breaking up with a fork as it cooks. When all traces of pink have disappeared, remove with a slotted spoon to paper toweling to drain. Pour off fat remaining in saucepan and discard.

3. Add butter and onion to saucepan and sauté 2 minutes. Stir in flour until well blended. Stir in wine and milk and cook, stirring, until thickened. Cook 1 minute.

4. Take off the heat and stir in ½ cup of the cheese until melted. Add salt and pepper, macaroni, and sausage to the cheese sauce and mix gently.

5. Preheat oven or toaster oven to 350 degrees.

6. Turn the macaroni mixture into a 1-quart baking dish or 2 individual au gratin dishes; sprinkle with remaining cheese and bake 20 minutes or until bubbly hot.

LINGUINE WITH WHITE CLAM SAUCE

You will have most of the ingredients for this tasty dish on hand; add a salad, some crusty bread and Buttered Pears in Cream (page 204), and dinner will be ready in less than 30 minutes.

1 tablespoon vegetable oil
1 clove garlic, finely chopped
¼ cup chopped parsley
½ cup chicken broth
1 can (8 ounces) minced clams, drained, with juice reserved
6 ounces linguine
2 tablespoons dry vermouth
Freshly grated Parmesan cheese

1. In a medium-size saucepan heat the oil and sauté the garlic 1 minute. Add parsley, broth, and clam juice. Bring to a boil; reduce heat and simmer, uncovered, 10 minutes.

2. Cook the linguine according to label directions only until *al dente* (cooked but not soft); drain and turn onto 2 deep plates.

3. Add vermouth and reserved clams to saucepan; reheat and pour over pasta. Sprinkle with Parmesan cheese.

For another delicious pasta dish, see

LINGUINE WITH SCALLOP SAUCE

in Fish

NO-FUSS RICOTTA AND
SPINACH "RAVIOLI"

■

Many people have been credited with discovering that wonton wrappers make terrific ravioli, so this is not a first, but it is an easy way to make the dish. As one package of wrappers contains 24 skins, it is sensible to use all and make four servings. The uncooked "ravioli" can be frozen on a cookie sheet and transferred to a plastic bag for storage to be ready for an almost instant meal at some future date. Add a salad and your favorite dessert for a quick meal.

1 tablespoon butter or margarine
1 shallot, finely chopped
2 ounces mushrooms (4 medium), finely chopped
½ polybag fresh spinach or ½ pound fresh, trimmed, washed,
*   and drained*
1 cup ricotta
1 tablespoon chopped fresh parsley
Pinch of ground nutmeg
2 tablespoons freshly grated Parmesan cheese
Pepper
1 package (1 pound) wonton wrappers
1 egg, lightly beaten
2 cups Well-Seasoned Tomato Sauce (page 187)
Parmesan cheese

1. In a small skillet heat the butter and sauté the shallot until tender but not browned. Add mushrooms and cook, stirring, until the moisture they give up has evaporated. Place spinach in large saucepan; cover and cook over low heat until wilted. Drain and press out excess liquid.

2. In a medium-size bowl combine the spinach, ricotta, parsley, nutmeg, Parmesan, and pepper. Mix well.

3. Take the wrappers out of the package and cover with damp towel. Remove 2 wrappers; place 1 tablespoon ricotta mixture in middle of one wrapper; brush egg in circle around filling; place second wrapper on top and seal where egg is. With a round biscuit cutter that just fits inside wrapper, cut a circle through egg seal.

Discard excess wrapper. Reserve "ravioli" and repeat with remaining wrappers.

4. Cook the "ravioli" in a large kettle of boiling water in batches of 12, if using all, for 1 minute. Drain well and reserve.

5. Preheat oven or toaster oven to 375 degrees.

6. Heat tomato sauce and pour half into a shallow baking dish. Arrange cooked "ravioli" on top of sauce. Pour over remaining sauce; sprinkle with Parmesan cheese and bake for 10 minutes or until bubbly hot.

Note: To serve two, put ½ cup of the sauce in 2 individual au gratin dishes; top with half the "ravioli" and another ½ cup of the sauce; sprinkle with Parmesan and bake in a preheated 375-degree oven for 10 minutes. Freeze remaining "ravioli" for another meal.

LINGUINE PRIMAVERA and

ELBOW MACARONI WITH CHEESE SAUCE

in Meatless Main Dishes

are other delicious pasta dishes

ZITI WITH SALAMI AND YELLOW SQUASH

This is a hearty and satisfying main dish to enjoy with a tossed green salad and Orange-Glazed Oranges (page 202) for dessert.

1 tablespoon olive oil
2 large scallions, chopped
¼ pound mushrooms, sliced
3 ounces Genoa salami, diced
1 cup Well-Seasoned Tomato Sauce (page 187)
½ cup frozen peas
¼ cup freshly grated Parmesan cheese
2 tablespoons chopped fresh parsley
1 small yellow squash, cubed
8 ounces ziti

1. In a medium-size skillet heat the oil and sauté the scallions and mushrooms 3 minutes. Add salami, tomato sauce, peas, Parmesan cheese, and parsley. Bring to boiling.

2. Steam the yellow squash 2 minutes; plunge into ice water; drain and add to sauce.

3. Cook the ziti according to label directions until *al dente;* drain and return to the hot pan. Add the sauce and toss to coat. Serve at once with more freshly grated Parmesan cheese.

SAUCES, FILLINGS, AND ACCOMPANIMENTS

WELL-SEASONED TOMATO SAUCE

■

I keep this sauce in the freezer in 1-cup quantities in boil-in-the-bags to make thawing easy. At the peak of the fresh tomato season, I use peeled, seeded, and chopped tomatoes (1 quart) in place of the canned, and in winter I make use of the tomatoes I have canned. Makes about 3 cups.

2 tablespoons olive or vegetable oil
2 large onions, finely chopped
2 large carrots, finely chopped
2 cloves garlic, finely chopped
1 can (2 pounds 3 ounces) Italian plum tomatoes
Salt and pepper
2 teaspoons leaf oregano, crumbled
3 tablespoons chopped fresh basil or 1½ teaspoons leaf, crumbled.
¼ cup chopped fresh parsley

1. In a large kettle heat the oil and sauté the onion until tender. Add carrots and garlic and cook, stirring often, for 4 minutes.

2. Add tomatoes, salt, pepper, oregano, basil, and parsley. Bring to a boil and simmer, uncovered, 30 minutes or until desired consistency.

BLENDER MUSHROOM SAUCE

✕ ⊙

This is a quick-to-make sauce that is good with chicken, fish, and vegetables such as cauliflower. I often double or quadruple the recipe and serve it as a soup.

¼ pound mushrooms (6 to 8), chopped (1⅓ cups)
½ cup diced celery
½ cup finely chopped shallot or scallion
½ cup milk
Salt and pepper
1 tablespoon butter

1. Place mushrooms, celery, shallot, milk, salt, and pepper in a small saucepan; bring to a boil; cover and simmer 8 to 10 minutes or until celery is tender.

2. Transfer the mixture to an electric blender and whirl until smooth; add the butter and whirl to mix.

SAUCE SUPREME

A pleasant sauce for chicken or fish which lends itself to the addition of fresh or dried herbs

1 tablespoon butter or margarine
1 tablespoon flour
¼ cup chicken broth
2 tablespoons half-and-half or heavy cream
2 tablespoons dry white wine or vermouth
Salt and pepper
1 teaspoon brandy

1. In a small saucepan heat the butter and blend in the flour and cook, stirring, 1 minute.

2. Stir in the broth, cream, and wine and bring to a boil, stirring. Cook, stirring, 1 minute. Stir in salt, pepper, and brandy.

BRANDIED PEAR APPLE SAUCE

Serve warm with game, poultry, or pork and ham dishes.

2 tart, flavorful apples, peeled, quartered, and cored
1 pear, peeled, quartered, and cored
⅓ cup dry white wine
⅓ cup cider or apple juice
Powdered sugar to taste
Cinnamon to taste
2 tablespoons brandy

1. Place apples, pear, wine, and cider in a medium-size saucepan. Cover pan and simmer until fruit is soft. Puree mixture in an electric blender or food processor; return to clean pan.

2. Stir in sugar and cinnamon and simmer, uncovered, until mixture is very thick, stirring often. Stir in brandy.

RAISIN SAUCE

An old-fashioned sauce that will keep indefinitely in the refrigerator if you wish to double or triple the recipe. Great for gifts. Serve with plain ham, pork, or tongue.

¼ cup water
½ cup sugar
¼ cup raisins
1 tablespoon butter or margarine
1 tablespoon cider vinegar
1 teaspoon Worcestershire sauce
Salt and pepper
¼ teaspoon ground nutmeg
¼ cup grape or currant jelly

1. In a small saucepan combine water and sugar; bring to a boil and stir to dissolve the sugar.
2. Add the raisins, butter, vinegar, Worcestershire, salt, pepper, nutmeg, and jelly and cook, stirring, until jelly has melted and the mixture is well blended and slightly thickened.

CANDIED CRANBERRIES

A decorative and piquant accompaniment for any fowl or game. Keep bags of cranberries in the freezer for year-round enjoyment.

½ cup fresh cranberries
¼ cup sugar
¼ teaspoon ground ginger
2 tablespoons grated orange rind

1. Preheat oven or toaster oven to 350 degrees.
2. Place berries in a small ovenproof dish. Sprinkle with sugar, ginger, and rind; cover and bake for 1 hour, stirring 3 or 4 times. Serve at room temperature.

DUXELLES OF MUSHROOMS
✕ ◉

This is a very thick mushroom stew or spread which makes a great filling for crepes, chicken breasts (see Chicken Breasts Duxelles, page 67), artichoke bottoms, and savory cream puff appetizers. Double the recipe and store in small quantities in tiny containers in the freezer for up to two months.

½ pound mushrooms, finely chopped
2 shallots, finely chopped
5 tablespoons butter
2 tablespoons flour
¼ cup half-and-half or heavy cream
Salt and pepper

1. The food processor makes chopping the mushrooms and shallots an easy task. Heat the butter in a skillet and sauté mushrooms and shallots over low heat until dark in color and almost dry, about 15 minutes.

2. Sprinkle with flour and cook, stirring constantly, 1 minute. Add cream and stir to mix well; cook 2 minutes or until thickened. Season with salt and pepper. Cool.

REFRIED BEANS

◉ ■

Prepare a whole pound of beans at one time because they freeze well in boilable bags for a quick side dish for Chicken Tacos (page 74) and Turkey Enchiladas (page 80). Or add chopped scallions and seeded chopped canned chilies to cold beans for a cracker and crudité spread or on tortilla chips for nachos.

1 pound dried pinto or pink beans
Water
1 medium-size onion, chopped coarsely
⅓ cup lard or ⅔ stick margarine
Salt
1 large onion, finely chopped
2 cloves garlic, finely chopped

1. Pick over and wash beans. Place in a bowl and cover with cold water and let soak at room temperature overnight.

2. Next day drain the beans and place in a large saucepan with 3 cups fresh cold water, coarsely chopped onion and 2 tablespoons of the lard or margarine. Bring to a boil, cover, and simmer for 40 minutes or until beans are almost tender. Add about 1 teaspoon of salt or to taste, cover, and cook 30 minutes longer, adding more water if needed.

3. Drain beans and reserve liquid. Heat remaining lard or margarine in a large skillet and sauté finely chopped onion and garlic until soft but not browned.

4. Add the beans to the skillet and mash into the onion with a potato masher. Add some of the reserved liquid if necessary to make a fairly smooth paste.

BASIC CREPES

∎

Make ahead and store in the freezer for an Instant Crepe Dessert (page 210) or Curried Chicken Crepes (page 70).

3 eggs
1½ cups milk
2 tablespoons vegetable oil
1 cup all-purpose flour
¼ teaspoon salt (optional)

1. Place all ingredients in the container of an electric blender in the order they are listed and whirl until smooth, scraping down sides of container as needed. Refrigerate up to 2 hours.

2. Heat a 7- to 8-inch skillet; grease lightly with shortening. Test consistency of batter; it should be like heavy cream. Thin with water, if necessary.

3. Pour 3 tablespoons into the hot skillet and tilt pan to spread evenly. When lightly browned, turn and brown the other side.

4. Stack crepes between double layers of wax paper. Cool. Wrap tightly in aluminum foil and freeze for up to 3 months.

Note: With double wax paper between crepes, you can easily remove the exact number you want without thawing. Recipe makes 12 to 14 crepes.

DESSERTS

APPLE ALMOND TARTS

✕ ☀ ■ ❦

This is a make-ahead dessert for a special occasion and, if you wish, you can double the recipe and freeze the two extra tarts for another day.

PASTRY:
4 tablespoons butter
½ cup flour
2 tablespoons 10X (confectioners) sugar

FILLING:
2 tablespoons almond paste or ground almonds
2 small apples
1 tablespoon butter
1 tablespoon sugar
1 egg yolk
⅓ cup milk or heavy cream
½ teaspoon vanilla

1. Preheat oven or toaster oven to 350 degrees. Place butter, flour, and 10X sugar in a bowl and mix with the fingers until crumbly. Press into two 4-inch tart pans* and chill quickly in the freezer while making the filling.

2. Spread almond paste over bottom of chilled tart shells. Peel, core, and slice the apples into ⅛-inch slices. Heat the butter in a medium-size skillet. Add apple slices and sprinkle with sugar. Sauté, tossing gently, for 5 minutes or until the fruit is almost transparent and tender. Cool. Remove apple slices to tart pans.

3. In a small bowl beat together the egg yolk, milk, and vanilla. Stir in butter/sugar mixture from skillet and pour over apples.

Place tart pans on a cookie sheet and bake 30 minutes or until firm and puffy. Serve slightly warm or at room temperature.

Note: If you double the recipe, use the leftover whites in the Frozen Chocolate Dessert (page 208).

* I use 4½×1¼-inch aluminum foil tart pans.

APPLE CRISP

I use my two favorite individual-size au gratin dishes for this dessert and they fit in the toaster oven or alongside another dish or roast in a regular oven. They can be cooked at 350 degrees or 325 degrees for a longer period, if it is more convenient. They are done when nicely browned and crusty on the top and the apples have cooked through.

6 apples, peeled, cored, and sliced.
1 tablespoon lemon juice
2 tablespoons brown sugar
¼ teaspoon ground cinnamon

TOPPING:
¾ cup all-purpose flour
¼ cup butter or margarine
¼ cup brown sugar
1 teaspoon ground cinnamon

1. Preheat oven or toaster oven to 350 degrees.
2. In a medium-size bowl toss the apples with lemon juice, brown sugar, and cinnamon and divide between two buttered au gratin or individual shallow baking dishes.
3. In the same bowl place the flour and butter and with the fingertips work the butter into the flour until it is the consistency of coarse oatmeal. Add the brown sugar and cinnamon and mix well. Spoon over the apples and bake for 35 minutes. Serve warm.

VIENNESE APPLE SOUFFLÉ

⊙

Serve with a hearty soup such as Bean and Spinach Soup (page 15) or light main dish such as Scallops in White Wine (page 37) for a delightfully different dinner. Prepare ahead through step 2 and have all other ingredients ready to finish off and bake 3 to 5 minutes between courses. Great for a light brunch.

1 tablespoon butter
1 large apple, peeled, cored, and cut into rings or slices
4 tablespoons sugar
2 eggs, separated
1 teaspoon grated lemon rind
½ teaspoon vanilla
1 teaspoon flour*

1. Preheat oven to 475 degrees. A toaster oven is not large enough. Heat butter to bubbling in an 8-inch (measured on the bottom) ovenproof skillet. I use my omelet pan. If handle is not ovenproof, wrap in aluminum foil. Add apple rings in one layer and turn to coat both sides. Sprinkle with 1 tablespoon of the sugar.

2. Sauté until apples are tender and slightly caramelized, turning once.

3. Meanwhile, beat the egg yolks with a fork until frothy, adding lemon rind and vanilla.

4. Beat egg whites until stiff and glossy, gradually adding remaining sugar combined with flour.

5. Quickly fold whites and yolk mixtures together and pile lightly over apple rings.

6. Bake for 3 to 5 minutes or until top is lightly browned. Turn upside down on serving plate. Serve at once.

* When my flour ran out, I substituted pancake mix.

BAKED STUFFED APPLES

Substitute 1 tablespoon raisins for the dates, if you prefer.

2 Rome Beauty or Cortland apples
2 pitted dates, diced
2 pecans or walnuts, chopped
2 teaspoons brown sugar
Dash of ground cinnamon
1 tablespoon frozen orange juice concentrate
½ teaspoon grated orange rind
2 tablespoons honey
1 tablespoon butter or margarine

1. Preheat oven or toaster oven to 400 degrees.

2. Core apples and, with the tip of a paring knife, score or pierce the skin all around the middle of the apple to avoid wrinkling and splitting.

3. In a small bowl combine dates, pecans, sugar, and cinnamon. Use the mixture to stuff apples.

4. Place apples in baking dish. Combine orange concentrate, rind, and honey and spoon over apples. Dot with butter.

5. Pour hot water into the dish to a depth of ¼ inch. Bake for 30 minutes; cover with aluminum foil and bake 10 to 20 minutes longer or until tender. Serve warm or at room temperature.

FLAMBÉED BANANAS

A last-minute dessert to fix between the courses.

2 bananas
2 tablespoons unsalted butter
2 tablespoons orange juice
1 tablespoon grated orange rind
2 tablespoons rum or orange-flavored liqueur

1. Peel bananas; cut in half lengthwise and again crosswise.

2. Heat butter and orange juice in a skillet; add bananas; cook over medium heat, turning often, until bananas are soft but not mushy. Sprinkle with orange rind.

3. Warm rum and pour over bananas; ignite and spoon liquid over bananas until flame dies down.

HOT LEMON SOUFFLÉ

A fine finish for a simple dinner of, say, Oyster Stew (page 35) or Veal Piccata (page 111). Put the soufflé in the oven as you sit down for the main course; it will be ready in 30 minutes.

⅓ cup sugar
3 eggs, separated
Grated rind of ½ medium-size lemon*
Juice of half a lemon
½ teaspoon cream of tartar
Pinch salt

1. Preheat oven to 350 degrees. A toaster oven is not big enough. Butter bottom and sides of a 1-quart soufflé dish and sprinkle with 1 tablespoon of the sugar.

2. With a whisk beat egg yolks in a bowl, gradually beating in remaining sugar, rind, and juice.

3. Beat whites until foamy; add cream of tartar and salt and beat on high speed until stiff and glossy. Fold one-third of the whites into the yolk mixture; pour this mixture over remaining whites and fold together gently. Turn into prepared soufflé dish. Place dish in pan with 1 inch hot water.

4. Place pan on middle shelf of oven and bake 30 minutes until well risen and just firm. Serve immediately.

* I prefer tart lemon desserts, so I use grated rind of one whole lemon.

ORANGE-GLAZED ORANGES

A make-ahead dessert that looks pretty and tastes great.

1 large navel orange
3 tablespoons orange-flavored liqueur
1 tablespoon sugar

1. Using a zester, remove the orange-colored rind from half the orange; reserve. With a sharp knife remove the white pith from orange; discard.
2. Slice orange crosswise into wheels. Combine liqueur and sugar in small saucepan. Bring to boil and boil until sugar is dissolved and mixture is syrupy. Pour over orange slices and sprinkle with reserved orange rind. Refrigerate.

FROZEN ORANGE MOUSSE

This recipe makes enough for three or four servings but that is a bonus to have in the freezer; also, the recipe may be doubled for even more frozen assets.

2 egg whites
6 tablespoons sugar
½ cup heavy cream
4 tablespoons orange-flavored liqueur
Grated rind of 1 small orange (about 1 tablespoon)
1 can (about 11 ounces) mandarin oranges in light syrup

1. Beat whites until foamy; beat in 2 tablespoons of the sugar very gradually until mixture is stiff and shiny.
2. Whip cream until soft peaks form; whip in 2 tablespoons sugar and stir in 2 tablespoons liqueur.
3. Fold whites and orange rind into cream mixture. Turn into 3 to 4 individual ramekins or freezer-safe dishes. Cover and freeze several hours or overnight.

4. Drain mandarin oranges and place syrup in a small saucepan with remaining 2 tablespoons sugar. Reduce to ⅓ cup by boiling hard. Cool. Stir in remaining liqueur and pour over mousse when serving; garnish with mandarin orange sections.

Note: Leftover mandarin orange sections can be used in a salad or as a garnish for ham.

PEACH SYLLABUB

A true summer dessert to make when the peaches are at their best.

2 large ripe peaches
2 tablespoons brandy
2 tablespoons honey
⅓ cup heavy cream
¼ cup 10X (confectioners) sugar
1 egg white

1. Drop peaches into boiling water for the count of five. Remove to ice water and slip off skins. Halve, remove pits, and slice into a bowl.
2. Combine brandy and honey and stir into peaches to coat all slices. Cover tightly and refrigerate.
3. Just before serving, whip cream until it holds soft peaks, gradually adding half the sugar.
4. Beat egg white until stiff while gradually adding remaining sugar. Fold cream and egg white mixture together and pour over fruit. Serve at once.

BUTTERED PEARS IN CREAM

A great dessert any time of the year because there are always fresh pears in the market. Just make sure they are not too ripe.

2 firm ripe pears
1½ tablespoons butter or margarine
1½ tablespoons sugar
2 tablespoons orange-flavored liqueur
2 tablespoons heavy cream

1. Halve pears; peel and core. Heat butter in a medium-size skillet until it bubbles. Add pears and sprinkle with sugar. Cook about 5 minutes on each side, basting with butter and sugar.

2. When pears are tender and sugar is beginning to brown, remove pears to serving dishes.

3. Add liqueur and cream to skillet; bring to boil, stirring. Pour over pears. Serve warm or at room temperature.

PEARS IN APRICOT SAUCE

This recipe will work with good quality canned pears; they will only need heating in the sauce.

1 cup fresh-squeezed orange juice
2 tablespoons apricot jam
4 whole cloves
1 piece (1 inch) cinnamon stick
2 lemon slices
1 tablespoon sugar
2 firm ripe pears, peeled, halved, and cored
Lemon slices

1. In a medium-size skillet combine the juice, jam, cloves, cinnamon, 2 lemon slices, and sugar; bring to a boil and simmer 10 minutes, stirring often.

2. Place pear halves cut side up in skillet and spoon orange mixture over them. Cover and cook 10 minutes or until pears are tender but not mushy. Spoon orange mixture over pears several times. Remove cloves and cinnamon stick. Serve warm, garnished with lemon slices.

RUSSIAN RASPBERRIES

This recipe is for the lucky few who have access to a cheap source of the scarce fruit or grow their own. The recipe can be halved if you only have 1 cup of the berries.

2 cups fresh raspberries
1 cup plain yogurt or sour cream
2 eggs
2 tablespoons sugar
1 tablespoon flour

1. Preheat oven or toaster oven to 350 degrees.
2. Spread raspberries over bottom of a 1-quart baking dish. Bake for 10 minutes.
3. In a medium-size bowl beat the yogurt, eggs, sugar, and flour together and pour over berries. Bake 35 minutes or until firm and golden. Serve warm or at room temperature.

STRAWBERRY MOUSSE

It is not practical to make less than four servings of this dessert but it will keep two to three days in the refrigerator and I'm willing to bet it won't stay there that long.

½ pint strawberries (about 9 medium-size)
1 teaspoon unflavored gelatin
2 tablespoons sugar
¼ cup water
1 egg white, at room temperature
¼ cup heavy cream, whipped

1. Wash and hull the berries and puree in an electric blender or food processor. Set aside.

2. In a small (pint capacity) saucepan mix the gelatin with 1 tablespoon of the sugar; stir in the water and allow to soften several minutes. Heat, stirring, until gelatin is dissolved.

3. Chill gelatin mixture until just before it starts to gel. Stir strawberry puree into gelatin mixture.

4. Beat the egg white until frothy; gradually beat in the remaining tablespoon sugar until soft peaks form. Fold strawberry mixture into egg white. Fold in the whipped cream and turn into four 8-ounce custard cups or dessert dishes. Chill.

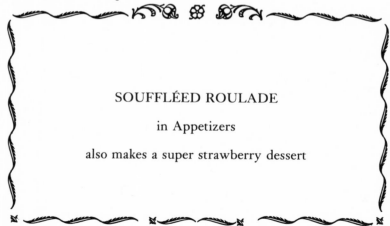

SOUFFLÉED ROULADE

in Appetizers

also makes a super strawberry dessert

FRUIT COMPOTE

Make several hours ahead to allow for chilling. Other berries can be substituted for blueberries.

½ cup blueberries
1 large ripe peach
2 tablespoons sugar or to taste
Dry red wine

1. Divide the blueberries between 2 bowls, sherbet glasses or balloon wine glasses.
2. Dip peach in boiling water for a count of five; remove and slip the skin off. Halve and remove pit. Place each half cut side down over berries.
3. Sprinkle with sugar and pour red wine to cover. Chill several hours.

SNAPDRAGONS

A simple three-ingredient dessert that is made ahead.

¼ cup golden raisins
2 tablespoons cognac or brandy
1 cup unsweetened, unspiced apple sauce

1. In a small saucepan combine the raisins and cognac. Heat to boiling; turn into a bowl and let stand overnight.
2. Fold raisins and juice into the apple sauce and spoon into dessert glasses. Serve with crisp cookies.

MAPLE RUM CUSTARD

Another make-ahead dessert that can be served as is or with fresh Fruit Compote (page 207) or stewed fruits.

1 cup milk
2 egg whites at room temperature
2 tablespoons maple syrup
1 tablespoon rum

1. Preheat oven or toaster oven to 325 degrees.
2. In a small saucepan heat the milk to scalding; little bubbles form around the edges of the pan.
3. Beat the whites until foamy; gradually beat in the maple syrup and when mixture is stiff, gradually pour in the hot milk while continuing to beat. Beat in the rum. Pour into two 10-ounce custard cups or baking dishes; set in a pan of hot water and bake for 25 minutes or until custard is set. Remove from water; cool; refrigerate.

FROZEN CHOCOLATE DESSERT

This recipe makes four servings and it is handy to have in the freezer. It is less rich than ice cream or mousse as it has no yolks and less cream.

½ package (6 ounces) semisweet morsels or ½ cup mini
semisweet morsels.
2 egg whites
Pinch of cream of tartar
2 tablespoons sugar
½ cup heavy cream
1 teaspoon sugar
½ teaspoon vanilla
¼ cup chopped toasted almonds

1. In a double boiler over simmering water melt the chocolate morsels. Cool slightly.

2. Beat egg whites with cream of tartar until frothy; gradually beat in the 2 tablespoons of sugar until stiff peaks form.

3. Beat the heavy cream with the 1 teaspoon of sugar until stiff. Fold in the vanilla and almonds; fold cream mixture and chocolate into the egg white mixture until no streaks of white remain. Turn into 4 custard cups; cover with plastic wrap, label, and freeze.

MOCHA MOUSSE

Make ahead and keep in the freezer for an emergency dessert. Double the recipe if you wish to store eight servings. It will keep in the freezer for three months.

¼ cup water
2 teaspoons instant coffee
3 ounces semisweet chocolate
3 eggs, separated
2 tablespoons coffee-flavored liqueur
3 tablespoons sugar
½ cup heavy cream, whipped

1. In a small saucepan combine the water, coffee, and chocolate and heat, stirring, until chocolate is melted and mixture is well blended. Beat egg yolks; gradually beat in coffee mixture. Add liqueur.

2. Beat the egg whites until foamy and gradually beat in the sugar until stiff peaks form. Fold the whipped cream into chocolate mixture; fold in whites. Turn into 4 freezer-proof ramekins. Freeze overnight or longer.

INSTANT CREPE DESSERT

It is instant if you have the crepes made ahead and stored in the freezer; just remember to thaw them.

2 tablespoons apricot jam
2 teaspoons brandy
6 Basic Crepes (page 193), thawed
2 tablespoons butter
¼ cup orange juice
1 tablespoon sugar
2 tablespoons orange-flavored liqueur
1 tablespoon grated orange rind
1 tablespoon slivered almonds

1. Combine jam and brandy in a small saucepan and heat gently until melted. Spread on crepes; fold crepes into quarters to form envelopes.

2. In a shallow skillet combine butter and orange juice. Heat, stirring, until steaming. Add crepes and spoon over sauce until heated through, about 3 to 4 minutes. Sprinkle with sugar and add liqueur.

3. Bring to a boil and serve hot, sprinkled with orange rind and almonds.

BREAD PUDDING WITH
WHISKEY SAUCE

This is soothing food that can be made ahead to serve with a vegetable soup such as Corn Chowder (page 18), a hearty appetizer such as Quick Pizza (page 9), or a main dish salad such as Ham and Lima Bean Salad (page 160), for a pleasant, light dinner.

2 slices firm white bread
1 tablespoon butter, softened
Orange marmalade or apricot jam
1 cup milk or half-and-half
2 eggs
2 tablespoons brown sugar
1 tablespoon grated orange rind
2 tablespoons golden raisins
1 tablespoon butter
2 tablespoons sugar
1 egg yolk
Bourbon whiskey or dark rum to taste

1. Preheat oven or toaster oven to 350 degrees. Remove crusts from bread; spread with butter and jam; cut slices into 4 triangles.

2. Heat milk in a small saucepan to simmering. Meanwhile, beat eggs with brown sugar and orange rind until foamy and gradually beat in the hot milk.

3. Place bread triangles around sides of 2 small heatproof bowls or two 10-ounce custard cups. Scatter raisins over bread and pour milk and egg mixture over all.

4. Place bowls in a pan of hot water. Bake for 30 minutes or until custard is set; remove from water and cool.

5. In a small saucepan combine butter and sugar and cook over low heat while stirring until sugar is dissolved and mixture is smooth. Cool slightly. Whisk in the egg yolk and cook until thick. Do not boil. Cool.

6. Add bourbon to taste and pour over custard; refrigerate.

INDEX

Almond Apple Tarts, 197–198
Amber Onion Slices, 140
Appetizers
  Asparagus, marinated, 129
  Avocado Halves with Spicy Sauce, 7
  Cheese, Herbed, 3
  Chicken liver (pâté), 76
  Clams Oreganato, 4
  Crab Spread, 4–5
  Pizza, Quick, 9
  Red Peppers, Roasted, with Anchovies, 8
  Salmon, Potted, 5
  Shrimp with Fennel, 6
  Souffléed Roulade with Mushroom Filling, 10–11
  Zucchini Quiche, Crustless, 11
Apple(s)
  Almond Tarts, 197–198
  Baked Stuffed, 200
  Crisp, 198
  and Ham, Rice Salad with, 177
  Sauce, Brandied Pear, 189
  sauce dessert (Snapdragons), 207
  Smoked Pork Chops with Red Cabbage and, 97
  Soufflé, Viennese, 199
Apricot and Rice Stuffed Cornish Game Hens, 56
Artichoke Hearts, Chicken Breasts with, 61
Asparagus
  marinated in Vinaigrette Dressing, 129
  Mimosa, 130

Ribboned, 129
  and scrambled eggs, 129
  and Snow Peas, Stir-Fried, 130–131
  Sole-Wrapped, 48
Avocado Halves with Spicy Sauce, 7
Avocado and Persimmon Salad, 165
Avocado, Sautéed, 131

Bananas, Flambéed, 200–201
Barbecued Chicken Breast, Oven, 62
Basic kitchen equipment, xiii–xvi
Bean(s)
  Baked, with Smoked Garlic Sausage, Quick, 101
  Green with Capers, 132–133
  Green, Parsleyed, 132
  Lima in Cream and Chives, 139
  Refried, 192
  and Spinach Soup, 15
  Tamale Pie, 125
Beef
  Cabbage, Stuffed, 93
  Meat Balls, 94
  Meat Loaf, Stuffed, 92
  Steak, Braised Chuck, 87
  Steak, Peppered Swiss, 88
  Stir-Fried Orange, 90–91
  Stir-Fried, Spicy, 89
Beet and Endive Salad, 163
Belgian Endive. See Endive
Black-Eyed Peas Salad, 157
Blender Mushroom Sauce, 188

Blue Cheese, Creamy Dressing,
170–171
Brandied Pear Apple Sauce, 189
Bratwurst in Beer, 116
Bread Pudding with Whiskey
Sauce, 211
Broccoli
Purée, 133
Shrimp with, Stir-Fried, 42
Soup, 16
Brussels Sprouts and Chestnuts,
148
Buttered Pears in Cream, 204
Butternut Squash, Baked, 148–149

Cabbage
with Caraway Seeds, Braised,
134
Cole Slaw with Peppers and
Pickles, 162
Red, and Apples, Smoked Pork
Chops with, 97
Stuffed, 93
Caesar Salad, 161
Candied Cranberries, 190
Cannellini, Bean and Spinach
Soup, 15
Cannellini Casserole, 135
Carrot Parsnip Purée, 140–141
Carrot, White Turnip and, 150
Cauliflower Soup, 16–17
Celery and Blue Cheese Soup,
Cream of, 17
Celery Sticks, 136
Celery sticks, Herbed Cheese in, 3
Cheese
Blue, Creamy Dressing,
170–171
Blue, and Celery, Cream Soup
of, 17
and Chick-Pea Salad, 158
Feta, with Shrimp, 41
Feta and Spinach, Ground
Lamb with, 105
Feta, Spinach, and Mushroom
Salad, 167
Fontina, with Bay Scallops, 38

and Ham Rolls, 103
Herbed, 3
and Macaroni, Super, 179
Parmesan Chicken Breasts, 68
Ricotta and Spinach "Ravioli,"
No-Fuss, 181–182
Sauce, with Elbow Macaroni,
123
-Stuffed Shells, 124
Chef's Salad, 155
Chestnuts and Brussels Sprouts,
148
Chick-Pea and Cheese Salad, 158
Chick-Pea and Smoked Turkey
Salad, 159
Chicken, A Perfect Roast, 53
Chicken Breast(s)
with Artichoke Hearts, 61
Cordon Bleu, 66
Curry, 72
Duxelles, 67
Greek, 64
with Mushrooms, 65
with Mustard and Cheese, 60
Oven Barbecued, 62
Parmesan, 68
Pot Pies, 70–71
Slightly Gamey, 58
Stir-Fried, 69
stuffed with Herbed Cheese, 3
Tacos, 74
with Wine and Herbs, 59
with Yoghurt, 63
Chicken (cooked)
Crepes, Curried, 70
Curry, 72
and Grape Salad, 156
Mousse, Hot, 73
Tacos, 74
Chicken Livers, Polenta with,
75–76
Chicken Livers Victoria, 76–77
Chicken, sauces for, 188–190
Chili, Turkey, 81
Chocolate Dessert, Frozen,
208–209
Chowder. See Soup

Cider Glazed Ham Steak with Yams, 102
Clam Chowder, Rhode Island, 18
Clam Sauce, White, Linguine with, 180
Clams Oreganato, 4
Cod, Baked with Fresh Tomato Topping, 31
Cole Slaw with Peppers and Pickles, 162
Compote, Fruit, 207
Confetti Rice, 177
Conversion Table, Metric, xix
Corn Chowder, 18–19
Cornish Game Hens
 Apricot and Rice Stuffed, 56
 Fruit Stuffed, 57
 in Port Wine, 55
 Roast, 54
 Sauces for, 189, 190
Crab Spread, 4–5
Cracked Wheat (Tabbouleh) Salad, 168
Cranberries, Candied, 190
Cream of Celery and Blue Cheese Soup, 17
Crepe Dessert, Instant, 210
Crepes, Basic, 193
Crepes, Curried Chicken, 70
Crustless Zucchini Quiche, 11
Cucumber Soup, Chilled, 19
Cucumbers, Ritz, 162
Curried Chicken Crepes, 70
Curried Lamb, 106
Curried Vegetables, 119
Curry, Chicken, 72
Curry, Shrimp, Creamy, 42–43
Custard, Maple Rum, 208

Desserts
 Apple Almond Tarts, 197–198
 Apple Crisp, 198
 Apple Soufflé, Viennese, 199
 Apples, Baked Stuffed, 200
 Bananas, Flambéed, 200–201
 Bread Pudding with Whiskey Sauce, 211
 Chocolate, Frozen, 208–209
 Crepe, Instant, 210
 Fruit Compote, 207
 Lemon Soufflé, Hot, 201
 Maple Rum Custard, 208
 Mocha Mousse, 209
 Orange-Glazed Oranges, 202
 Orange Mousse, Frozen, 202–203
 Peach Syllabub, 203
 Pears in Apricot Sauce, 204–205
 Pears, Buttered, in Cream, 204
 Raspberries, Russian, 205
 Snapdragons (raisin-apple-sauce), 207
 Souffléed Roulade (Strawberry), 10–11
 Strawberry Mousse, 206
Dilled Salmon Steaks, 36
Dressings. See Salad Dressings
Duck, Roast, with Fruit Stuffing and Sauce, 83–84
Dugleré. See Tomatoes
Duxelles, Chicken Breasts, 67
Duxelles of Mushrooms, 191

Eggplant with Garlic, Sautéed, 138
Eggplant Parmigiana, 137
Eggs, scrambled, and asparagus, 129
Elegant menus for company, xxi
Enchiladas, Turkey, 80
Endive and Beet Salad, 163
Endive and Watercress Salad, 163
Equipment, basic kitchen, xiii–xvi
Equivalents, Table of, xix–xx

Feta Cheese with Shrimp, 41
Feta Cheese and Spinach, Ground Lamb with, 105
Feta, Spinach and Mushroom Salad, 167
Finnan Haddie Dugleré, 32–33
Fish. See also Seafood
 Cod Baked with Fresh Tomato Topping, 31

Fish (*cont.*)
  Finnan Haddie Dugleré, 32–33
  Haddock with Dill Butter, 32
  Kedgeree (leftover), 33
  Salmon, Potted, 5
  Salmon Steaks, Dilled, 36
  Sauces for, 188
  Smelts, Pan-Fried, 45
  Sole in Champagne Sauce, 46
  Sole Kiev, 47
  Sole, Stuffed, 49
  Sole-Wrapped Asparagus, 48
  Swordfish, Butterflied and
    stuffed, 50
  Tuna with Marinated Vegeta-
    bles and Chick-Peas, 169
Flambéed Bananas, 200–201
Florentine, Scallops, 39
Flounder. *See* Sole
Fowl. *See* Poultry
French Onion Soup, 23
French Pizza, 120–121
Fried Rice, 175
Fruit. *See also name of fruit*
  Compote, 207
  Salad, Fresh, 164
  Stuffed Cornish Game Hens, 57
  Stuffing and Sauce for Roast
    Duck, 83–84

Game Hens. *See* Cornish Game
    Hens
Gamey Chicken, Slightly, 58
Gazpacho, 20
Grape and Chicken Salad, 156
Greek Chicken Breast, 64
Green Beans with Capers,
    132–133
Green Beans, Parsleyed, 132
Ground meat. *See* Beef, Lamb, etc.

Haddock with Dill Butter, 32
Haddock, smoked, Finnan Haddie
    Dugleré, 32–33
Ham
  and Apple, Rice Salad with, 177
  and Cheese Rolls, 103

and Lima Bean Salad, 160
sauces for, 189–190
Steak, Cider Glazed with Yams,
    102
Herb-Stuffed Potatoes, Twice-
    Baked, 145
Herbed Cheese, 3
Honey Yoghurt Dressing, 170
Hors d'oeuvres. *See* Appetizers

Instant Crepe Dessert, 210
Italian Sausages and Peppers with
    Spaghetti, 100

Kedgeree (leftover fish), 33
Kitchen equipment, xiii–xvi
Kitchen food staples, xvii–xix

Lamb
  Breast with Lentils, 109
  Chops Teriyaki with Rice, 110
  Curried (leftover), 106
  Ground (or leftover), with Feta
    Cheese and Spinach, 105
  Hotpot, 107
  Roast Leg of, 104
  Shanks, Braised, 108
Leek and Potato Soup, 25
Leeks, Braised, 138–139
Leftover combinations, xxii–xxiii
Lemon Rice, 178
Lemon Soufflé, Hot, 201
Lentil Soup, 21
Lentils, Lamb Breast with, 109
Lima Bean and Ham Salad, 160
Lima Beans in Cream and Chives,
    139
Linguine Primavera, 122
Linguine with Scallop Sauce,
    38–39
Linguine with White Clam Sauce,
    180
Liver. *See* Chicken Livers

Macaroni and Cheese, Super, 179
Macaroni, Elbow, with Cheese
    Sauce, 123

Main dish suggestions, xi–xii
Maple Rum Custard, 208
Marinated Asparagus, 129
Marinated Vegetables, 169
Meat. *See also* Beef, Lamb, Pork, etc.
Meat Balls, 94
Meat Loaf, Stuffed, 92
Meatless main dishes. *See also* Rice, Pasta, Salads, etc.
  Bean Tamale Pie, 125·
  Cannellini Casserole, 135
  Cheese-Stuffed Shells, 124
  Curried Vegetables, 119
  Eggplant Parmigiana, 137
  Elbow Macaroni with Cheese Sauce, 123
  French Pizza, 120–121
  Linguine Primavera, 122
  Marinated Vegetables with chick-peas and tuna, 169
  Zucchini Frittata, 120
Menu suggestions, xi–xii, xx–xxiii
Menus, elegant, for special occasions, xxi
Menus, leftover, xxii–xxiii
Metric Conversion Table, xix
Mr. Cornwall's Tomato Cobb (Cold Soup), 26
Mocha Mousse, 209
Mousse
  Frozen Orange, 202–203
  Hot Chicken, 73
  Mocha, 209
  Strawberry, 206
Mushroom(s)
  Chicken with, 65
  Duxelles of, 191
  Salad, 164
  Sauce (Soup), Blender, 188
  Soup, 22
  Spinach and Feta Salad, 167
  Stuffed with Herbed Cheese, 3
  Veal Stew with, 113
Mussels in White Wine, 34

Normandy Potato Salad, 166

Onion Slices, Amber, 140
Onion Soup, French, 23
Orange-Glazed Oranges, 202
Orange Mousse, Frozen, 202–203
Osso Buco, 114
Oyster Stew, 35

Parmesan Chicken Breasts, 68
Parsleyed Green Beans, 132
Parsnip Carrot Purée, 140–141
Pasta dishes
  Cheese-Stuffed Shells, 124
  Elbow Macaroni with Cheese Sauce, 123
  Linguine Primavera, 122
  Linguine with Scallop Sauce, 38–39
  Linguine with White Clam Sauce, 180
  Macaroni and Cheese, Super, 179
  Macaroni, Elbow, with Cheese Sauce, 123
  "Ravioli," Ricotta and Spinach, No-Fuss, 181–182
  Spaghetti, Sausage and Peppers with, 100
  Ziti with Salami and Yellow Squash, 183
Pea(s). *See also* Chick-Pea, Snow peas
  Black-Eyed, Salad, 157
  Petits Pois, Winter, 142
  Purée of, 141
  and Rice, Venetian Style, 142–143
  Soup, Split Pea, 24
  Summer Garden, 143
Peach Syllabub, 203
Pear(s)
  Apple Sauce, Brandied, 189
  in Apricot Sauce, 204–205
  in Cream, Buttered, 204
  Pork with, 94–95
Peppers
  Red, Roasted, with Anchovies, 8

Peppers (*cont.*)
  and Rice, Veal Stew with, 112
  and Sausage with Spaghetti,
    100
  Shrimp with, Stir-Fried, 44
Persimmon and Avocado Salad,
  165
Petits Pois, Winter, 142
Pizza, French, 120–121
Pizza, Quick (Spiedini), 9
Polenta with Chicken Livers,
  75–76
Pork
  Chops, Smoked, with Red Cab-
    bage and Apples, 97
  Cutlets Normandy, 96
  with Pears, 94–95
  sauces for, 189, 190
  Shredded, with Scallions and
    Sprouts, 98
  Spare Ribs for Two, 99
Potato(es)
  and Leek Soup, 25
  Salad, Normandy, 166
  and Sausage Skillet, 101
  Scalloped, 144
  Sweet, Patties, 149
  Twice-Baked, Herb-Stuffed,
    145
Potted Salmon, 5
Poultry. *See* Chicken, Turkey, etc.
Puréed Vegetables. *See name of*
  vegetable

Quiche, Zucchini, Crustless, 11

Raisin Sauce, 190
Raspberries, Russian, 205
Ratatouille, 146
"Ravioli," No-Fuss Ricotta and
  Spinach, 181–182
Recipe Symbols, xxiii, 91
Red Peppers. *See also* Peppers
Red Peppers, Roasted, with An-
  chovies, 8
Refried Beans, 192
Rhode Island Clam Chowder, 18

Rice
  and Apricot Stuffed Cornish
    Game Hens, 56
  Confetti, 177
  Fried, 175
  Lemon, 178
  and Peas, Venetian Style,
    142–143
  and Peppers, Veal Stew with, 112
  Salad, Cold, 176
  Salad with Ham and Apple, 177
  Wild, 178
Ricotta and Spinach "Ravioli,"
  No-Fuss, 181–182
Ritz Cucumbers, 162
Rock Cornish Game Hens. *See*
  Cornish Game Hens
Roulade, Souffléed, with Mush-
  room Filling, 10–11
Russian Raspberries, 205

Salads
  Asparagus, marinated, 129
  Caesar, 161
  Chef's, 155
  Chick-Pea and Cheese, 158
  Chicken and Grape, 156
  Cole Slaw with Peppers and
    Pickles, 162
  Cucumbers, Ritz, 162
  Endive and Beet, 163
  Endive and Watercress, 163
  Fruit, Fresh, 164
  Ham and Lima Bean, 160
  Mushroom, 164
  Peas, Black-Eyed, 157
  Persimmon and Avocado, 165
  Potato, Normandy, 166
  Rice, Cold, 176
  Rice with Ham and Apple, 177
  Spinach, Mushroom, and Feta,
    167
  Tabbouleh (Cracked Wheat),
    168
  Turkey, Smoked, and Chick-
    Pea, 159
  Vegetables, Marinated, 169

Salad Dressings
  Blue Cheese, Creamy, 170–171
  Honey Yoghurt, 170
  Vinaigrette, 171
Salami and Yellow Squash, Ziti
    with, 183
Salmon, Potted, 5
Salmon Steaks, Dilled, 36
Salt, use of, xii
Sauce
  Apricot, Pears in, 204–205
  Brandied Pear Apple, 189
  Cranberries, Candied, 190
  Mushroom, Blender, 188
  Raisin, 190
  Scallop, Linguine with, 38–39
  Supreme, 188
  Tomato, Well-Seasoned, 187
  Whiskey, Bread Pudding with,
    211
  White Clam, Linguine with,
    180
Sausage
  Bratwurst in Beer, 116
  and Peppers with Spaghetti,
    100
  and Potato Skillet, 101
  Smoked Garlic, Quick Baked
    Beans with, 101
  Turkey, Breakfast, 82
Scallop(s)
  Bay, with Fontina Cheese, 38
  Florentine, 39
  Fried Bay, 40
  Sauce, Linguine with, 38–39
  Seviche, 40–41
  in White Wine, 37
Scalloped Potatoes, 144
Seafood. See also Fish
  Clam Sauce, White, Linguine
    with, 180
  Mussels in White Wine, 34
  Oyster Stew, 35
  Scallop Sauce, Linguine with,
    38–39
  Scallops, Bay, with Fontina
    Cheese, 38

Scallops Florentine, 39
Scallops, Fried Bay, 40
Scallops in White Wine, 37
Seviche (scallop), 40–41
Shrimp Curry, Creamy, 42–43
Shrimp with Fennel, 6
Shrimp with Feta, 41
Shrimp with Peppers, Stir-
    Fried, 44
Shrimp, Stir-Fried, with Broc-
    coli, 42
Seviche, scallop, 40–41
Shopping suggestions, xvi–xvii
Shrimp
  with Broccoli, Stir-Fried, 42
  Curry, Creamy, 42–43
  with Fennel, 6
  with Feta, 41
  with Peppers, Stir-Fried, 44
Smelts, Pan-Fried, 45
Smoked Pork Chops with Red
    Cabbage and Apples, 97
Smoked Turkey and Chick-Pea
    Salad, 159
Snapdragons (apple sauce des-
    sert), 207
Snow Peas and Asparagus, Stir-
    Fried, 130–131
Snow peas, Herbed Cheese on, 3
Sole
  in Champagne Sauce, 46
  Kiev, 47
  Stuffed, 49
  -Wrapped Asparagus, 48
Soufflé, Lemon, Hot, 201
Soufflé, Viennese Apple, 199
Souffléed Roulade with Mush-
    room Filling, 10–11
Souffléed Roulade with strawber-
    ries, 10–11
Soup
  Bean and Spinach, 15
  Broccoli, 16
  Cauliflower, 16–17
  Celery and Blue Cheese, Cream
    of, 17
  Clam Chowder, Rhode Island, 18

Soup (*cont.*)
    Corn Chowder, 18–19
    Cucumber, Chilled, 19
    Gazpacho (cold), 20
    Lentil, 21
    Mushroom, 22
    Mushroom (Sauce), Blender,
        188
    Onion, French, 23
    Oyster Stew, 35
    Potato and Leek (hot or cold),
        25
    Split Pea, 24
    Tomato Cobb, Mr. Cornwall's
        (cold), 26
    Zucchini (hot or cold), 26–27
Spaghetti, Sausage and Peppers
    with, 100
Spare Ribs for Two, 99
Spiedini (Quick Pizza), 9
Spinach
    and Bean Soup, 15
    and Feta Cheese, Ground Lamb
        with, 105
    Mushroom and Feta Salad, 167
    and Ricotta "Ravioli," No-Fuss,
        181–182
    Scallops Florentine, 39
    Wilted, 147
Split Pea Soup, 24
Squash, Butternut, Baked,
    148–149
Squash, Yellow, and Salami, Ziti
    with, 183
Staples for kitchen, xvii–xix
Steak. *See* Beef, Ham
Stir-Fried
    Asparagus and Snow Peas,
        130–131
    Beef, Orange, 90–91
    Beef, Spicy, 89
    Chicken, 69
    Pork, Shredded, with Scallions
        and Sprouts, 98
    Shrimp with Broccoli, 42
    Shrimp with Peppers, 44
    Vegetables, 151

Strawberry Mousse, 206
Stuffed Cabbage, 93
Summer Garden Peas, 143
Sweet Potato Patties, 149
Swiss Peppered Steak, 88
Swordfish, Butterflied and
    Stuffed, 50
Syllabub, Peach, 203
Symbols for use of recipes, xxiii,
    91

Tabbouleh (Cracked Wheat
    Salad), 168
Tacos, Chicken, 74
Tamale Bean Pie, 125
Tarts, Apple Almond, 197–198
Teriyaki Lamb Chops with Rice,
    110
Tomato Cobb, Mr. Cornwall's
    (Cold Soup), 26
Tomato Sauce, Well-Seasoned,
    187
Tomatoes, Finnan Haddie Du-
    gleré, 32–33
Tongue, Raisin Sauce for, 190
Turkey
    Breakfast Sausage, 82
    Breast with Vegetables, Roast
        Half, 78
    Chili, 81
    Drumsticks, Braised, 79
    Enchiladas, 80
    Smoked, and Chick-Pea Salad,
        159
Turnip, White, and Carrot, 150
Twice-Baked, Herb-Stuffed Pota-
    toes, 145

Veal
    Piccata, 111
    Sausage and Peppers with Spa-
        ghetti, 100
    Sausages in Beer, 116
    Shanks, Osso Buco, 114
    Stew with Mushrooms, 113
    Stew with Peppers and Rice,
        112
Vealburgers, Stuffed, 115

Vegetable(s). *See also* name of
  vegetable
  Curried, 119
  Marinated, 169
  Ratatouille, 146
  Sauce, Blender Mushroom, 188
  Stir-Fried, 151
Viennese Apple Soufflé, 199
Vinaigrette Dressing, 171

Watercress and Endive Salad, 163
Weekend shopping and cooking,
  xvi–xvii
Well-Seasoned Tomato Sauce, 187
Whiskey Sauce, Bread Pudding
  with, 211

Wild Rice, 178
Wilted Spinach, 147
Winter Petits Pois, 142

Yams, Cider Glazed Ham Steak
  with, 102
Yoghurt, Chicken with, 63
Yoghurt Honey Dressing, 170

Ziti with Salami and Yellow
  Squash, 183
Zucchini
  Frittata, 120
  Limone, 150
  Quiche, Crustless, 11
  Soup, 26–27